Spicy Food

Also by Stendahl

Best Restaurants—New York

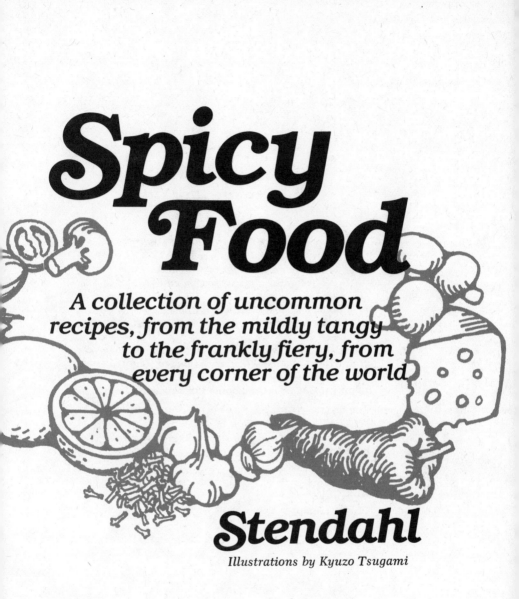

Spicy Food

A collection of uncommon
recipes, from the mildly tangy
to the frankly fiery, from
every corner of the world

Stendahl

Illustrations by Kyuzo Tsugami

Holt, Rinehart and Winston   New York

Published by Holt, Rinehart and Winston,
383 Madison Avenue, New York, New York 10017.

Published simultaneously in Canada by
Holt, Rinehart and Winston of Canada, Limited.

Library of Congress Cataloging in Publication Data

Stendahl.
    Spicy food, a collection of uncommon recipes,
from the mildly tangy to the frankly fiery, from
every corner of the world.

    Includes index.
    1.   Cookery.   2.   Spices.   I.   Title.
TX715.S83   641.6′3′84   79–11075
ISBN 0–03–015641–6

FIRST EDITION

Designer: Joy Chu
Printed in the United States of America
1   3   5   7   9   10   8   6   4   2

This book is dedicated to
Janet, Victoria, Gordon, and Lindsay,
whose ready hunger was a
constant inspiration.

*We have in this at the same time
the flavor of amber, cloves, nutmeg,
ginger, pepper and sweet herbs—
yet all so well balanced that the
presence of one does not injure
the flavor of the rest. How
delicious it is!*
—1001 Nights

Acknowledgments

Creating a book on spicy cooking around the world is a task that cannot be achieved without help and lots of it. My thanks and gratitude to the following, as well as many others:
Rickey Austin, Janet Bernal, Goldie Blanksteen, Madame Cecilia Chiang, Francis Cheong, Marie Deitch, Jane Flora, Virginia Molony Jackson, Tsuneo Kanazaki, Paul Kovi, George Lang, Harriet Lembeck, Tom Margittai, Sirio Maccioni, Kid Ory, Marjorie Thorson Parsons, Helen Roberts, St. Regis Hotel Bar, Louis Szathmary, Jean-Louis Todeschini, Jean Vergne, Tekle Woldemikael, Nicola Zanghi, Nino Zanghi.
. . . and with special thanks to Eileen Mercer, and to B. Bailey Marcus, who nobly toiled to make an *oreille de porc* out of the sow's ear of my scribbles. And of course to Ellyn Polshek and Susan Arensberg, editors with plenty of spice.

Contents

Preface

The basis of this book is recipes from my personal file, garnered over years of wonderful eating, around the world and at home. The remaining recipes have been gleaned from every culture where spices are held in esteem—and that means most countries. I assure you that most of the recipes in this book are not easily obtainable in print elsewhere.

This is not a specialist's cookbook, but it shouldn't be your first cookbook either, although even beginners will find most of the recipes easy to make. The more you appreciate good food and good cooking, the more inventive you can become, using this book as your starting point.

So, be adventurous—and if you improve on a recipe, or find a new one that is worthwhile, please send me the results for my next book.

It is important here not to confuse the sainted word "spice" with the mundane word "hot." A few spices do sting the tongue, but the majority give a dish breadth, depth, and a subtle enrichment.

Nothing so damages the thrill of expectation as a dish that promises to be piquant and turns out to be bland. Most of the recipes in this book will benefit from an extra pinch of whatever bewitching spice provides their soul; I have been conservative only out of a sense of avuncular protection for those who are welcoming spices into their lives for the first time.

In conclusion, remember this: unseasoned ground pork fries up into cooked pork. Add enough of the right spices and you end up with an unforgettable sausage.

It's all a matter of taste.

Stendahl

September 1979

Spicy Food

About Spices, Particularly Peppers

Many definitions have been offered to separate spices from herbs. They are both vegetable products used to add flavor and interest to cooking. Spices generally come from warmer climates than herbs do. That is one reason why we have no Eskimo recipes in this book. It likewise explains why there are so many eggplant recipes, since the mad apple proliferates in warm climates. (It also happens to be one of my passions; I consider the eggplant edible blotting paper because it so beautifully absorbs many different kinds of flavors.)

Since spices add pungency and lilt, and since both veal and fish are exceptionally delicate in flavor, there are few veal or fish dishes included. Spices and sweets in combination do not seem to appeal to Western palates, so there are also few desserts here. There is plenty of everything else.

Spices start with allspice (so named because of its complex flavor), continue through the lily family (onions, garlic, and chives), and end with the orchid (vanilla). Most complete spice lists total about fifty in number. Almost all of them you will find used in the recipes in this book.

The earliest known use of spices dates back to the building of the pyramids, somewhere around 2500 B.C. We know that onions and garlic were fed to the laborers to keep up their strength.

The first known Western cookbook, written by Apicius in the

first century A.D., shows that the Romans adored spices and imported them from every part of their known world.

In medieval days spices again came into their own, but not, as some believe, to preserve meat. Poor men ate fresh meat as they killed it. It was the rich who enjoyed gamy meats at their banquets. And as part of their show of pomp and power, they hired the best cooks they could. In turn, the cooks showed off by concocting incredible dishes that called for every sort of surprising spicy combination.

As final comment in this whirlwind spice history, I'd like to point out that the New World was discovered accidentally by men seeking a route to the sources of the great spices. Vasco da Gama, Columbus, and all the rest were looking for spices, not territory. Their goal was a shortcut to the legendary Spice Islands, which were the Moluccas, in Indonesia. Our continent merely happened to be in the way.

Storing spices. The aromatic oils that give spices their liveliness tend to evaporate. Try to buy spices in small quantities and always keep them in jars with tight lids. Store away from heat. Dried varieties in leaf form are far more flavorable than commercially powdered forms. And grinding a spice fresh will always immensely improve the dish.

Grinding spices. It is more convenient to use commercially powdered spices, but it is more fun to grind your own, and the results will be measurably better. Spices may be ground in a mortar and pestle, in an old-fashioned coffee grinder, in a blender or food processor, or even crushed between waxed paper with the bottom of a bottle. I have invested in a little electric spice grinder that works beautifully. Cinnamon bark, turmeric, and cardamom seeds are tough items to crack; it is far simpler to make an exception and obtain these three spices already powdered.

Measuring spices. Never pour spices from an open-mouthed jar. Pour a little into the inside of the lid, then take as many pinches as you need from that. Or use a measuring spoon.

What to do for too much spice. It is difficult to do anything, which is why careful measurement is important.

- Try adding a peeled, quartered potato to the overseasoned mix.
- Add rice or pasta, if the dish lends itself to such additions.

- The best solution is to build up the dish with more of everything except the spices.
- *A dish should never taste of one predominant spice.* It is better to underspice than to overdo your enthusiasm.

Of all the precious herbs and spices that made men risk lives and kingdoms, the greatest is pepper. Pepper is also the most confusing, since there are two totally unrelated spices called pepper, and both are beloved around the world.

The two basic types of pepper are:

- the true black peppercorn (or pepperberry) identified as *Piper nigrum.*
- the large family that includes paprika, cayenne, and all of the varieties of chilies (variously spelled chillies or chiles)—those chili peppers identified as *Capsicums.*

Piper Nigrum (Black Pepper)

Black pepper is and has always been a favorite of every Western culture, and is used—sometimes in several different forms in the same dish—as whole peppercorns, cracked, coarsely ground, or finely ground, in nearly every kind of cooking except sweet desserts. It is even used in a few of those.

Black peppercorns originated on the steamy Malabar coast of India. Many claim that Tellicherry corns, or berries, from Malabar are still the world's finest, even though the little black berries are now grown in tropical zones around the world.

When Alaric the Visigoth besieged Rome in the fifth century, a major part of the ransom he demanded was 30,000 pounds of black pepper. In the Middle Ages, dock workers who unloaded pepper had to wear special pocketless uniforms so they could not take home a few mementos.

Peppercorns are pungent and aromatic, and when freshly milled or cracked they yield a delectability unlike any other spice in the world. Peppercorns should be stored in a cool place (your refrigerator is best) in a tight-capped container—just like coffee beans, and for the same reason. They should always be ground fresh at the instant of need. Desiccated pepper ground commercially and packed in tins is simply a hot powder that makes you sneeze; fresh-milled pepperberries give warmth, aroma, flavor, and magic.

White pepper is the sun-dried pepperberry minus its pungent outer coating. This pepper is less strong, but otherwise identical. Chefs use it in white sauces, because it becomes invisible; personally I like seeing black specks before my eyes.

Green peppercorns are unripe berries packed in brine or wine vinegar. Those from Madagascar are considered the best, and experts warn that you should buy only those packed in cans, where their flavor remains intact. Since they are light-sensitive, *poivre vert* packed in jars will deteriorate on the shelf. Of late it has become a habit to use these mild, immature berries to flavor duck dishes.

Mignonette is an old-fashioned term for ground pepper and other spices tied in a muslin bag to be steeped while a dish is being cooked.

There are at least two other popular spices that by their appearance seem to belong to the *Piper nigrum* family but do not —allspice and Szechuan pepper.

Allspice comes from the berry of the pimenta, a West Indian tree. Its flavor is a little like a combination of nutmeg, cinnamon, and clove. The major source of allspice is Jamaica, and the next time you hear the term "Jamaica pepper," you'll know that it's really allspice.

Szechuan peppercorns, which have a reddish brown color, look and taste somewhat like a cross between allspice and black pepper, although they have a tang all their own. I urge you to experiment with them outside of Chinese cooking; for instance, try substituting them for black peppercorns. These berries are not to be confused with Szechuan chilies, which are small dried hot red peppers of the *Capiscum* family.

Capiscums (Chili Peppers)

The second category of peppers are the green, yellow, or red pods that grow in many shapes and sizes—from blistery little cherries and inch-and-a-half fiery terrors to slim and curling mild Mexican peppers (green chilies), which are almost identical in appearance to Italian (green frying) peppers, and finally to the plump, gentle bell peppers.

This large family of peppers (over a hundred different

varieties) is an original American product, cultivated for centuries by the Indians before Columbus was surprised by their
piquancy and fire and brought samples home to Europe. Today
these green, yellow, and red beauties flourish in China, Japan,
India, Africa—indeed, every semitropical and tropical climate.

Although technically all these peppers are chili peppers, I
have called only one of them chili in this book: that slim green
pod so familiar in the Southwest, a close cousin to the California
Anaheim, and similar to the pale green frying pepper, which
also goes under the name Italian pepper. This Italian pepper is
not to be confused with the Tuscany pepper, which is a small
green culinary bomb.

The small, thin, curling peppers available in Latin American and Caribbean tiendas will in this book be identified as hot
fresh green peppers (or red or yellow). The dried ones (almost
always red) I will call simply dried red peppers. These small-
sized peppers are all blistering hot, and the tinier they are, the
more fire they contain.

Remember also that the greatest heat dwells in the seeds.
Whether the pepper is fresh or dried, discard the seeds and be
careful when you handle any kind of hot peppers—some people's skin becomes irritated by the oils they contain. Sensible
cooks wear rubber gloves when seeding or chopping a hot pepper and avoid touching hands to face. Always wash both gloves
and hands in soapy water immediately after handling hot chili
peppers.

One of the most common varieties of hot peppers is the
jalapeño, either fresh or canned. It is fiery when fresh but loses
its savor when canned. In fact, all the canned or bottled products
—labeled "Tuscany peppers," "Mexi-peppers," or *jalapeños*,
poblanos, *chipotles*, *serranos*, etc.—usually supply only heat
without flavor. Some of them are almost pure fire, so be wary.

The gentlest member of the *Capsicum* family is the bell
pepper (it is also commonly called a green pepper). It thrives
in a cool climate and when ripe turns red, but remains mild.

From two different varieties of the *Capsicum* family come two
famous powders used in cooking: paprika and cayenne.

Paprika. Contrary to superstitious noncooks who think anything red must be hot, paprika peppers yield a very mild powder for the most part, and are used chiefly for the color they add. A pinch of paprika brightens a pale rice or potato dish, and adds a rosy luster to the simplest broiled chicken.

Mexican and Spanish paprika are acceptable, but they are not as vivid as Hungarian paprika. Whatever the difference in cost, real Hungarian *paprickasch* is worth seeking out for its brilliancy and its taste. As an old Hungarian saying has it: "One man may yearn for fame, another for wealth—but everyone yearns for paprika goulash."

True to the complexity of peppers, there is more than one type of Hungarian paprika: a sweet paprika, which my Hungarian friends tell me is seldom used; a mild, the customarily used paprika; and a hot, also seldom used, which seems to taste identical to cayenne. Paprika, incidentally, is one of our best sources of vitamin C.

Cayenne. This comes from many places, but never from Cayenne, Guiana. (One authority states that there is a red-feathered canary that gains its colorful plumage from being fed cayenne pepper when young. How would that bird *taste?*) Cayenne is always a powder, made from various hot dried peppers, and it ranges from deep orange to fire-engine red. It supplies little savor but immense heat, and should be used respectfully. Many labels merely state "red pepper"—this means cayenne.

In addition to peppers, peppercorns, and the powders derived from them, there are many concoctions that include peppers in some form. Here are brief descriptions of those used often in the book.

Chili powder is a mixture of ground dried chili peppers, garlic, oregano, cumin, and salt. Southwest Americans create a great variety of chili powders, ranging from "chocolaty" to blistering. Supermarket chili powder has too much filler and too little character. Seek your source in a Latin American, Caribbean, or Oriental shop. Or buy it by mail from a shop listed in the back of this book.

Tiny red or green peppers cured in vinegar. Many specialty stores stock tiny red or green peppers cured in vinegar. They are all *hot*. It is good to use the flavored liquid in stews or salad dressings and keep refilling the bottle with fresh white vinegar.

Chili sauce. Common supermarket chili sauce is generally a type of catsup doctored with more sugar and possibly a dash of horseradish or garlic powder. It is worthy of nothing more than hot dogs or hamburgers.

Hot sauce, or hot pepper sauce, is another general-purpose condiment that can range from a commercial tomato sauce faintly tinged with spice to slim bottles that are (or simulate) preparations from Louisiana or the West Indies. Vinegar, salt, and sometimes sugar (in West Indian versions) are blended with a chili pepper purée.

Tabasco sauce. Of all versions of red or green fire in vinegar, not one compares to Tabasco sauce in elegance and refinement. This patented formula is made from tiny flame-hot Louisiana peppers, aged and liquefied and slightly calmed in a light vinegar base. Compare Tabasco with any similar sauce and you will find it worth its extra cost. Tabasco is not a luxury, because a drop or two is sufficient. I use it less to make a dish peppery than to employ one drop of its subtle magic to smooth out and give a glow to a soup or gravy. It is a catalyst, like the lemon peel in a martini.

There are recent hot sauce arrivals from Taiwan and the People's Republic of China to be experimented with. These are called "hot sauce," "Szechuan hot paste," "chili (or chile) sauce," "hot oil," etc. Most are interesting variations of hot peppers plus either bean paste or oil. They are usually tongue-tinglers.

Note on Measurements

Feel free to substitute or adjust in all of the recipes, using any pepper seasoning you like best. Cayenne or dried red pepper flakes are often easiest to control in measuring.

If you are a novice, try these equations as a start:

one 1½-inch dried red pepper, ground in a mortar
  = ¼ teaspoon cayenne
  = ⅓ teaspoon dried red pepper flakes
  = 4 shakes (not drops) Tabasco or other liquid pepper
    sauce.

Sauces, Chutney, and Mustard

A few other categories of spicy condiments that are used in this book have nothing to do with peppers.

Fish sauce. The ancient Romans were mad for a liquid called *garum,* or *liquamen,* made from putrefied fish entrails, plus vinegar and pepper. Apicius and others hint that it was far more complex than that, and it was so admired a concoction that several Roman factories turned it out in great quantity.

In Southeast Asian cuisines there is a popular liquid used today called fish sauce, or *nuoc mam.* Although it contains anchovy, the sauce is not at all fishy in taste, but salty, rather like a sophisticated soy sauce. This condiment is not hot, only piquant and zestful (see p. 234).

Worcestershire sauce. A British colonial who returned from India in the last century tried to have English chemists recreate a bottled liquid he had become fond of out there. The attempt failed, and a barrel of the stuff lay forgotten in the chemists' cellar. Several years later, the two chemists, a Mr. Lea and a Mr. Perrins, discovered the barrel, liked the taste of the aged brew, and bottled it. Famous as Worcestershire sauce, it is somewhat like a modern *garum.*

A-1, House of Parliament, Bull Dog, and various other English or Oriental "steak sauces" or "catsups" are basically liquid chutneys, modified so as not to startle Western palates. They are insipid products compared to genuine chutneys.

Chutney. A condiment blended of sugar, fruits, vegetables, and spices, chutney comes to us from India. British colonials liked to serve a chutney with meat—hence the chutneylike steak sauce derivatives mentioned above. Many people think that Major Grey Chutney is generic, but it is only one of countless types, which can include apples, bananas, lemons, celery, or eggplant, among other ingredients, in chunk, bits, or puréed.

Major Grey is a popular variety of sweet mango chutney, a blend of mango pieces, raisins, vinegar, ginger, salt, and sugar. Another chutney type, a favorite of mine, is Bengal Club, a spicy-sweet purée. (See p. 159 for a recipe for a typical mango chutney.)

Authentic Indian shops also sell *pickles,* based on essentially the same ingredients as a chutney but without sugar and with a large amount of salt and a staggering amount of hot pepper. If there were such a thing as dynamite jam, an Indian pickle would be it.

Dry mustard. This is also called "English mustard," although it is of Chinese origin. *Wasabi*, sometimes labeled "horseradish powder," is a Japanese equivalent, but is green instead of yellow. Both powders should be mixed with a little liquid (stale beer or Oriental rice vinegar is best). Wasabi is best served at once; Chinese mustard should sit about 15 minutes. Neither should be saved for reuse, because they quickly lose their savor. Some premixed varieties of "Chinese mustard" are on the market. They are expensive and nowhere as good as the simply concocted real thing.

Spice Blends

In the heyday of classic French cuisine, chefs often created their personal secret spice blends, used with great discretion but pervasively, so that each dish they created bore the subtle mark of their own special style, a culinary signature.

I think this is going too far, but it can be fun to work up a casserole or other dish with a haunting, indefinable taste. I include, therefore, a few spice blends here, and I hope you will experiment with new combinations of your own.

 Quatre Épices
Four Spices

This is a classic French spice mix, which can be used to heighten the taste of anything but desserts.

    1 cup ground white pepper
    4 tablespoons freshly grated nutmeg
    3½ tablespoons powdered ginger
    1½ tablespoons powdered cloves

MAKES ABOUT 1½ CUPS

℀ Spice Blend After Carême

This spicy mix is formulated after that of Antonin Carême, the "cook of kings and the king of cooks," whose twelve-volume work in the early nineteenth century first codified the principles of *la haute cuisine*. All the ingredients should be pounded fine in a mortar or put through a grinder *before* measuring.

3 parts peppercorns (white and black in equal measure)

1 part each:
bay leaf
powdered cinnamon
whole cloves
powdered ginger
mace
freshly grated nutmeg
thyme

Work the ground mixture through a coarse sieve and store corked tightly. Use very sparingly in soups, stews, and casseroles.

℀ Mignonette, or Nouet

A modern approximation of an old-time French spice mix. It will sharpen the flavor of hearty casseroles, stews, and soups.

1 part each:
whole cloves
coriander seed
cumin seed
powdered ginger
dried red pepper flakes

Grind the spices separately, and then blend them by the spoonful in equal amounts. Sew by teaspoonfuls in bags made of muslin.

To use, steep a bag in a stew, soup, or casserole dish. Discard the bag before serving the dish.

🎵 Chinese Five-Spice Powder

An ancient and pungent mix to be used only occasionally and then sparingly. It has a pronounced flavor that goes well in many Chinese dishes, particularly those based on duck. A tiny pinch will also brighten most barbecue sauces. The ingredients are obtainable in Chinatown singly or already mixed, or see Mail-Order Sources.

> *1 part each:*
> powdered cinnamon
> whole cloves
> fennel seed
> star anise
> Szechuan peppercorns

Grind the spices separately before measuring, then mix well and store in an airtight jar.

🎵 Calexico Seasoning for Poultry and Meats

Of Mexican descent, this mixture is easy to prepare. It keeps well and is splendid to rub on grilled meats and poultry before or during cooking.

> ⅔ cup salt
> 2 tablespoons freshly ground black pepper
> 2 tablespoons chili powder
> 1 tablespoon cayenne
> 1 tablespoon garlic powder

Mix well and store in an airtight jar.

MAKES APPROXIMATELY 1 CUP

⅋ Rub-on Spices for Roasts

This recipe makes a thick rub-on mixture, but the addition of a little more olive oil and some light wine makes it into a most satisfactory marinade for a leg of lamb or a roast of pork. Omit rosemary when the meat is beef.

    1 clove garlic, minced
    6 juniper berries, cracked
    1 teaspoon crushed rosemary
    ½ teaspoon seeded and minced dried red pepper
    ½ teaspoon grated lemon peel
    freshly ground black pepper
    4 tablespoons olive oil
    1 tablespoon lemon juice

Crush all dry ingredients, being generous with the black pepper. In a small bowl, continue to grind and crush the ingredients as you add, a few drops at a time, first the oil and then the lemon juice. This makes a pestolike paste (not a liquid). Rub the paste well into the meat. Wrap loosely in waxed paper, or put meat into a plastic bag, and place it in a bowl. Let meat season in the refrigerator for several hours, or overnight. Roast as usual. If desired, you can dissolve any leftover marinade in dry vermouth and use as a baste.

MAKES MARINADE FOR
A 4- TO 6-POUND ROAST

⅋ Rosy Salt

Adds fiery zip to a boiled egg, and peps up a dull piece of meat.

    1 heaping tablespoon salt
    1 tablespoon Hungarian paprika
    1 teaspoon cayenne

Mix ingredients well and store in a jar with a tight lid. Use only a very small pinch at a time.

MAKES ABOUT 3 OUNCES

ℜ Stendahl's Spice Blend

Inspired by Escoffier, this is a mixture to be kept within arm's reach at the stove. Use it sparingly, to scent, not to overpower. If you have no scale, use teaspoons rather than ounces. It will be a different mix, but equally useful.

6 ounces black peppercorns
3 ounces celery seed
3 ounces powdered ginger
3 ounces freshly grated nutmeg
2 ounces thyme
2 ounces coriander seed
1 ounce garlic powder
1 ounce Hungarian paprika
1 ounce whole cloves
½ ounce cayenne
½ ounce juniper berries
½ ounce rosemary
4 or 5 bay leaves

Grind all ingredients to a fine powder in a mortar—using a blender is cheating, but it saves time. Pass through a coarse sieve, and store in an airtight jar.

MAKES 1 QUART

ℜ Stendahl's Fifteen-Spice Curry Powder

Years ago, while browsing through a curious book of chemical formulae, among recipes for making soap, dissolving rust, and bleaching linens, I found one for making curry powder. It was so exciting in taste that I eagerly thumbed every Indian source-book I could lay hands on, trying to find a more "authentic" recipe. I have always returned gratefully to what I now consider to be one of the world's best curry powders. Indian friends over the years have tended to agree with me.

True, Indian cooks carefully grind distinctly different blends from a palette of some thirty or more spices, so that every dish has its own subtle flavor combination. But even Indians use basic ready mixes, sometimes. What we label curry powder they call *garam masala*.

Garam masala should not be confused with *garum*, a type of fish sauce that is discussed on p. 8.

Do me the honor of never using a commercial curry powder or a tinned *garam masala* in making any recipe in this book.

Stendahl's Fifteen-Spice Curry Powder is essential to making a good curry (see recipes). The tiniest pinch will also enliven a salad dressing, make boiled or scrambled eggs into a sophisticated luncheon dish, and can be rubbed lightly on poultry, pork, or lamb before barbecuing. A hearty pinch will also transform a simple tomato soup into a exotic potage.

  8 ounces powdered turmeric
  8 ounces coriander seed
  8 ounces cumin seed
  6 ounces powdered ginger
  4 ounces black peppercorns
  2 ounces shelled cardamom seed or 1 ounce powdered
     cardamom
  2 ounces fennel seed
  2 small dried red peppers, seeded and minced
  2 ounces powdered mace
  1 ounce whole cloves
  1 ounce mustard seed (yellow)
  1 ounce poppy seed
  1 ounce garlic powder
  1 ounce fenugreek seed
  1 ounce cinnamon bark or ½ ounce powdered cinnamon

After grinding all ingredients that need it mix everything together in a big bowl. (Wear a gauze mask if you can find one at your drugstore. These spices give off potent fumes.) The perfume of this curry will improve with age, as long as it is kept in absolutely airtight jars. Filling many 2- or 4-ounce jars is better than storing in one or two large jars.

MAKES ABOUT 2 QUARTS

Ras el Hanout

In Morocco, each spice shop has its own particular blend of spices, along with enough other spices to make our own local stores look bare. These special blends are called *ras el hanout* or "top of the shop." If you want to make your own simplified *ras el hanout*, start with a good strong and pungent curry powder (see Stendahl's Fifteen-Spice Curry Powder). Add a little dried mint and some exotics such as allspice, dried lavender (if you can find it at an herbal shop), and some crushed dried rose petals. In other words, aim for a spice that is hot, faintly sweet, and very fragrant. Whatever you come up with will be the merest hint of a true *ras el hanout*—most of which have as many as thirty or forty different spices, some of them unavailable to us.

Use your *ras el hanout* as you would a super-curry powder: add a dash to salad dressings and stews, or rub it into meats before cooking, and so on.

What to Drink with Spicy Cooking?

If you bite into a blistery pepper and your throat begins to sear, the best thing to do is *not* to drink anything, but to take a mouthful of rice, or a bit of bland potato, pasta, or bread.

As to what beverages go well with piquant cookery, the classic saying is that the best wine for spicy foods is beer. It is true that the tangy effervescence of an icy beer refreshes the palate during a peppery meal as nothing else seems to. But there are other appropriate beverages.

Two schools of thought prevail. One prescribes something bland, such as tea, milk, or a drink such as *lassi*, an Indian refresher of thinned yogurt, flavored with rose water, sweetened or salted. The second school fights fire with fire, suggesting that a sturdy beverage will stand up against the strong taste of lip-tingling foods. Good hot coffee is an example.

As to wines, I believe that various cuisines demand different types. For spicy Oriental dishes, California, German, or particularly Alsatian Rieslings make fine companions. A Chenin Blanc from California or a white Zinfandel also seems suited to Chinese foods. For piquant, rather than hot, foods, Swiss Neuchâtel, French Vouvray, or a dry light Zinfandel rosé seems right to me.

And of course one of the heavier-bodied French champagnes should turn any feast into a banquet.

With some spicy fish, a flinty chablis might be appropriate, and meals that feature chicken or shellfish might call for an Alsatian Riesling, or any of the spicier German wines. The Italian Pinot Grigio also possesses enough character to stand up against these foods.

With red meat dishes, a robust red wine is indicated. A husky châteauneuf-du-pape, a mellow Burgundy, or a full-bodied St.-Émilion are choices I've made with enjoyable results.

For sturdier spicy meat dishes I prefer Italian wines. These are not only robust enough to match peppery foods, but they are also currently among the best wine bargains available.

Chianti Classico or Classico Riserva is a splendid table companion to a well-spiced meal. Chiantis from the heartland of Tuscany are entitled to be called Classicos. When a Classico is superior enough in quality so that the vintner ages it a minimum of three years, it is entitled to be called a Riserva. Wines from other parts of Italy that are aged up to four years or more before being bottled have also earned the Riserva classification. These are a bit more expensive than the rest, but are the best buys.

Wines from northern Italy, the Piedmont and Lombardia, are big wines that age well and often fill the room with their perfume.

Look for aged wines with these labels: Barolo, Barbaresco, Barbera, Dolcetto, Gattinara, Ghemme, Brunello, Inferno, Sassella, and Spanna.

Two special Italian favorites that are sufficiently full-bodied to tame almost any spicy cooking, Amarone and Sfursat, are stocked only in first-class wine stores, but they are worth searching out.

Finally, if you have any doubts, stick to well-chilled beer or water.

To end and top a well-spiced meal, try a good Cognac or Armagnac, black coffee, or a cappuccino. And if a suave port or cream sherry fails to put out the flame, it will in any case enhance the occasion.

Appetizers

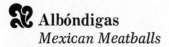 **Albóndigas**
Mexican Meatballs

These go very well with cocktails. In their alternate version they spark up a good beef broth as a starter for a Mexican meal.

Chorizo is obtainable at Latin food shops. Spanish chorizo is more expensive than domestic, but superior. If chorizo is unavailable, make your own (see Homemade Chorizo) or substitute ½ pound ground beef, blended with 1 tablespoon imported paprika, ¼ teaspoon cayenne, and at least 1 clove of garlic, minced.

> ½ pound chorizo (about 3 links)
> 1½ pounds ground beef
> 1 teaspoon salt
> 1 small onion, grated
> 1 egg, beaten
> 1 tablespoon powdered cumin
> ¾ cup fine bread crumbs
> 2 tablespoons olive oil
> ½ cup red wine (optional)
> 1 cup Fresh Tomato Sauce (p. 227, optional)

Remove skin from chorizo and mix well with beef. With fingers, mix in salt, onion, egg, cumin, and crumbs. Shape into balls, the size of golf balls. Sauté in oil, turning gently with wooden spoon to brown. For appetizers, add wine and tomato sauce and simmer 10 minutes.

SERVES 6 TO 12

𝕏 Spicy Cocktail Balls

Hors d'oeuvres are usually categorized as Hot or Cold, but we can also divide them into Delicate and Hearty. These robust tidbits definitely fall into the Hearty category.

> 1 pound ground beef
> 1 pound ground lean pork
> 2 tablespoons chili powder
> 1 tablespoon cumin seed
> 1 clove garlic, minced
> ½ teaspoon thyme
> ½ teaspoon salt
> generous grinding black pepper
> Barbecue Sauce (pp. 229–230)

Preheat oven to 300° F. Combine all ingredients except barbecue sauce, mixing well. Shape into tiny balls. Bake on an ungreased cookie sheet for 20 minutes. Place meatballs in a chafing dish to keep warm, and cover with heated barbecue sauce.

SERVES 15 TO 20

𝕏 Lamojen, American-Style

Lamojen is a kind of Armenian pizza. A California Armenian woman taught me this simplified American version, which substitutes beef for lamb. This dish, like the familiar pizza, can be served in large slices or individual rounds for dinner or in small slivers as an hors d'oeuvre. Pita, Middle Eastern flat bread, is obtainable in Oriental groceries and in many supermarkets.

1 pound ground beef
35-ounce can tomatoes, drained
1 large bell pepper, seeded and finely chopped
1 small bunch fresh parsley, minced
salt, freshly ground black pepper, generous pinch cayenne
6 to 8 pita or English muffins

Mix all ingredients except bread in a large bowl—hands are better than any other tool. Be sure the tomatoes are drained of all liquid possible, or the dish will be spoiled. Preheat broiler.

Separate the pita top from bottom, or split English muffins with a fork. Slice each pita or muffin into thirds or fourths.

Spread a thin layer of the meat mixture on each flat bread surface. Broil until meat is cooked—about 3 minutes. Eat while smoking hot.

SERVES 12 TO 16 AS HORS D'OEUVRES

ℵ Sausage Biscuits

These savory little biscuits will disappear quickly at cocktail time. They can be prepared and baked ahead of time, then frozen.

1 pound bulk sausage (or Home-Style Sage Sausage, see
recipe)
2 cups Bisquick or use only dry ingredients from biscuit
recipe, p. 253
8 ounces extra-sharp cheddar cheese, grated
½ teaspoon dried red pepper flakes

Heat oven to 400° F. Combine all ingredients, working sausage and cheese to mix well. Shape into small balls and place on ungreased cookie sheet. Bake until golden brown, about 25 minutes. Serve piping hot. If cooked and frozen, remove from freezer and heat at 350° F. for 15 minutes.

SERVES 8 TO 10

℘ Spicy Bacon Roll-Ups

These tasty little hors d'oeuvres are made up in advance, an added advantage for the busy host.

>   4 slices bacon, cooked and crumbled
>   2 ounces sharp cheddar cheese, finely grated
>   1 egg, beaten
>   1 teaspoon butter
>   ¼ teaspoon dry mustard
>   ¼ teaspoon Hungarian paprika
>   dash salt
>   dash Tabasco
>   4 slices white bread

Place all ingredients except bread into a bowl, and mix to form a paste. Trim crusts from bread and roll slices with rolling pin until very thin. Spread each slice generously with paste, and roll up bread. Wrap rolls in waxed paper and chill for at least 1 hour. To serve, heat broiler or toaster-oven to high temperature (450°F.). Unwrap and slice each roll into four or five rounds. Place on ungreased baking sheet and toast until brown, about 5 minutes. Serve skewered on toothpicks.

MAKES 16 TO 20

℘ Sour Bacon

Of German origin, this dish is not at all sour, but it is piquant. It is one of those always-welcome items that can be served either as an hors d'oeuvre on crackers or as a main dish over rice.

>   2-pound slab lean bacon, diced
>   8 onions, finely chopped
>   ¼ cup white vinegar
>   ¼ cup water
>   1 tablespoon sugar
>   dash Tabasco
>   generous sprinkling Hungarian paprika

In a large skillet, cook bacon until crisp, then pour off most of fat. In the residue left in skillet, sauté onions until translucent. Add vinegar, water, and sugar and simmer until sauce thickens to gravy consistency, stirring all the while. Add Tabasco. Before serving, dust generously with paprika. (The dish may be served either hot or cold.)

SERVES 10 TO 15 AS AN HORS
D'OEUVRE, 4 TO 6 AS A MAIN DISH

Cocktail Wieners with Cumberland Sauce

This is a simple recipe, easily prepared ahead and reheated. But don't let its simplicity deceive you: the tangy flavor and heady aroma will have your guests returning to the serving table for seconds—and thirds.

2 pounds cocktail or regular wieners

Simple Cumberland sauce
10-ounce jar currant jelly
½ cup fresh orange juice
8-ounce jar Dijon mustard
¼ teaspoon powdered ginger (optional)
1 orange peel, grated
1 lemon peel, grated
1 cup port

If using regular wieners, cut them into bite-size pieces.

Mix remaining ingredients in saucepan and cook over low heat until jelly melts. Cool to room temperature.

Simmer wieners in boiling water 5 minutes. Drain.

To serve: Put a toothpick into each bite of wiener, and keep them in a chafing dish. Set dish of sauce beside the dish. Guests dip as they wish. You may store extra sauce in freezer.

SERVES 18 TO 20

⅋ Chicken Wings with Ginger

These wings are a sure hit at cocktail hour. They are best when served fresh from the flame, but they're delicious any time.

> 1 pound chicken wings
> ¾ cup dry sherry
> ¼ cup soy sauce
> 2 cloves garlic, mashed
> 2 tablespoons minced fresh ginger
> ½ teaspoon powdered ginger
> 1 egg
> ½ cup flour, plus extra to dust chicken
> 1½ cups vegetable oil

Marinate the chicken wings for 4 hours in a mixture of the sherry, soy sauce, garlic, and ginger, turning occasionally. Make a batter by mixing together the egg and ½ cup flour with ⅓ cup of marinade. Pour oil into deep skillet or pot and heat until very hot (about 360° F.). Drain the wings, dust them with flour, and dip into the batter. Fry the wings a few at a time until golden brown—about 10 minutes.

SERVES 4 TO 6

⅋ Fried Bananas, Amazon-Style

Try this exotic nibble at your next cocktail party in place of the ubiquitous potato chip.

> ⅓ cup orange juice
> ⅓ cup yellow cornmeal
> 4 firm bananas
> ½ cup vegetable oil
> ½ teaspoon salt
> freshly ground black pepper
> dash Tabasco
> 2 ounces pimiento

Pour orange juice and cornmeal into separate bowls. Slice peeled bananas into ⅛-inch rounds. Moisten banana rounds in orange juice, and roll them in cornmeal to coat. In a skillet, heat oil over a medium-high flame. Fry bananas until lightly browned, a handful at a time. Remove from skillet with a slotted spoon, drain on paper towels, and arrange on a serving platter.

Toss banana slices very lightly with salt, a generous grinding of pepper, and Tabasco. Slice pimiento into thin strips, and decorate the platter. Serve warm, or at room temperature.

SERVES 4

ℜ Creole Oysters

Here is a celebrated New Orleans appetizer. Make sure your oysters are the largest and freshest available.

    14 oysters in the shell
    1 tablespoon butter
    1 whole scallion, minced
    2 tablespoons flour
    dash salt
    dash nutmeg
    dash cayenne
    1 heavy shaking Worcestershire sauce
    pinch finely chopped fresh parsley
    1 teaspoon Dijon mustard
    3 ounces fresh mushrooms, finely chopped
    1 egg yolk, slightly beaten
    rock salt or kosher salt
    ½ cup cracker crumbs
    1 tablespoon butter, melted

Heat oven to 350° F. Remove oysters from shells carefully, reserving 14 shells and ⅓ cup of the liquid. Wash and chop the oysters. Wash the shells.

In a large skillet, melt the 1 tablespoon butter over medium heat and sauté scallion. Blend in flour, stirring constantly, until mixture is bubbly. Slowly add oyster liquid, salt, nutmeg, cayenne, Worcestershire, parsley, mustard, and mushrooms. Add oysters and cook 3 minutes, stirring constantly. Remove from flame and add the beaten egg yolk. Arrange oyster shells in pie tins layered with rock salt. Fill the shells with the oyster mixture. Blend cracker crumbs with melted butter, and sprinkle over the oysters. Bake for about 15 minutes.

SERVES 3 TO 4

℘ Spiced Mushrooms

Perky little mouthfuls for the cocktail hour or as a prelude to lunch.

> 1 pound medium mushroom caps (save stems for other uses)
> white wine vinegar to cover (about 1 cup)
> 2 whole scallions, finely minced
> 1 large bay leaf
> 3 whole cloves
> 1 clove garlic, minced
> dash Tabasco
> salt and freshly ground black pepper
> vegetable oil (about ½ cup)

Place cleaned mushroom caps in bowl and cover generously with wine vinegar. Refrigerate for at least 1 hour. Drain mushrooms and place in a jar. Add scallions and other seasonings. Pour in just enough oil to cover mushrooms. Close jar tightly, shake gently, and refrigerate for 2 days.

SERVES APPROXIMATELY 8

℘ Guacamole

From Mexico, this popular concoction has won its way to all parts of America and possibly the world, or at least wherever the pear-shaped avocado grows. It may be served as a dip, on crisp-fried tortillas, on crackers, or even on a lettuce leaf as a salad. Guacamole does not store well unless you seal it with a layer of olive oil.

    1 avocado, peeled and mashed
    1 large ripe tomato, peeled and finely chopped
    1 teaspoon fresh lemon juice
    1 clove garlic, mashed
    1 tablespoon finely chopped onion
    2 dashes Tabasco
    ¼ teaspoon cumin seed

Combine all ingredients and mash to a paste.

SERVES 4

🎵 Pickled Eggplant

A succulent temptation from the Middle East, delectable hot or cold.

    1 large or 2 medium eggplants
    ⅓ cup olive oil
    6 cloves garlic
    1 tablespoon Hungarian paprika
    large pinch cayenne
    1 rounded teaspoon powdered cumin
    2 tablespoons red wine vinegar

Cut eggplant into long thin strips, leaving peel attached. Steam for 12 minutes. (If you lack a regular steamer, place strips on a rack suspended over lightly boiling water.) If wet, pat dry. Heat oil over high flame in a deep skillet, and add garlic. When garlic cloves are soft, mash with fork, then discard. Put eggplant strips in the oil, and add paprika, cayenne, and cumin. Cook uncovered, turning often, until eggplant is lightly browned and very soft— about 6 minutes. Add the vinegar and cook 1 minute longer.

Chill and serve cold with cocktails. Can also be served hot as a vegetable with a main dish.

SERVES 12

ℵ Welsh Rarebit

The Swiss made the fondue famous, even though the Chinese and the Japanese and the Mongolians had known about it for centuries. Then the English adapted it in typical fashion, making their fondue heavier and heartier and adding a whimsical name.

    2 large eggs
    1 heaping teaspoon dry mustard
    1 teaspoon Worcestershire sauce
    generous dash Tabasco
    dash salt and freshly ground black pepper
    1 cup warm beer (or milk, if you're a sissy)
    1 pound sharp cheddar cheese, diced
    1 teaspoon flour
    ¼ cup good dry sherry
    toast or crackers
    Hungarian paprika

Beat the eggs lightly, and add the seasonings and beer or milk. Mix well, and set aside. In a double boiler, melt the cheese, and blend in flour, stirring constantly. Blend egg mixture into cheese and beat with a whisk until thick, but do not overcook. Just before serving, stir in the sherry. Serve on toast or on crackers, dusting each serving with paprika.

SERVES 4

ℵ Rinktum Diddie

This is not the chorus of a folk song, but an old American appetizer, a cousin to the fondue and the soufflé. I like the name. Toasting the crackers in the oven or frying them, buttered, until golden improves the dish.

2 tablespoons butter
2 tablespoons flour
¾ cup light cream
1½ cups chopped fresh tomatoes
⅛ teaspoon baking soda
1 teaspoon salt
dash Hungarian paprika
dash cayenne (2 dashes if you live on the frontier)
dash freshly grated nutmeg
2 cups grated cheddar cheese
2 eggs, lightly beaten
about 16 buttered salted crackers

In saucepan, melt the butter over low heat and add flour, stirring about 1 minute. Gradually add the cream, tomatoes, baking soda, and all seasonings. Raise heat to medium and stir constantly until thickened. Lower heat and stir in the cheese. When cheese has melted, remove pan from heat. Stir in eggs and serve quickly, spooning onto crackers.

SERVES 4 TO 6

 Curried Deviled Eggs

Rare is the deviled egg that really tastes spicy. This recipe adds a fillip of curry.

6 hard-boiled eggs, peeled and halved lengthwise
1 tablespoon fresh lemon juice
¼ cup melted butter
½ teaspoon dry mustard
1 teaspoon grated onion
1 rounded teaspoon curry powder (p. 13)
dusting Hungarian paprika

Carefully remove yolks from eggs, and press them through a sieve or Mouli grater. Reserve whites. Mix the yolks, lemon juice, butter, mustard, onion, and curry powder. Spoon the mixture back into the egg whites. Dust each half with paprika. Chill until ready to serve.

MAKES 12 HALVES

ℜ Tex-Mex Vegetable Cocktail

What Texans did before the blender was invented, I do not know. But when that handy appliance came along, they did right by it with this refreshingly tangy before-dinner drink.

>12 ounces fresh green beans
>1½ cups tomato juice
>1 small clove garlic, finely minced
>dash Tabasco
>dash salt

Wash green beans, and remove ends. Put all ingredients in the blender and blend for 30 seconds, or until smooth.
This can be served either hot or very cold.

MAKES 3 CUPS

ℜ Tea Eggs

These make a highly unusual cocktail accompaniment. They are a kind of imitation Chinese "thousand-year-old" egg with a slightly salty, subtly smoky taste. Depending on how thoroughly the shells are crackled, the surfaces will be either mottled or a uniform chocolate-brown.

>8 to 12 eggs
>3 tablespoons black tea leaves
>2 tablespoons soy sauce
>1 tablespoon salt
>1 star anise, separated into cloves

Cover eggs with cold water. Bring to a boil, stirring occasionally to center the yolks. Reduce heat and simmer gently for 12 minutes. Remove the eggs and reserve the water. Cool the eggs under cold running water until you can handle them comfortably. Roll each egg gently to crackle the shell. Do not remove the shell. Bring reserved water to a boil, adding more if necessary to make 3 cups. Add tea leaves, soy sauce, salt, anise, and the crackled eggs. Cover and simmer until shells turn dark brown—about 1 hour. Turn off heat and let eggs stand covered for 2 hours. Drain, shell, and rinse the eggs. Chill and serve quartered.

The eggs will keep for several days, refrigerated, if they are left unshelled and in the liquid in which they were cooked.

SERVES 8 TO 12

🎵 Deviled Almonds

These almonds are devilishly good at cocktail time; they make the next round taste even better.

    1 cup unsalted almonds
    1 tablespoon butter
    large pinch salt
    ¼ teaspoon cayenne

If almonds still have their skins, blanch them: put them in a small bowl, pour in enough boiling water to cover, and let stand for about 2 minutes. Drain off water and add cold water. Remove almonds one at a time and squeeze to pop off the skin. Dry on paper towels.

Heat butter in a skillet and sauté nuts lightly until golden brown. Drain on paper towels. Sprinkle liberally with salt; add cayenne. When cool, shake off surplus seasonings. These will keep crisp if tightly sealed.

MAKES 1 CUP

𝕏 Watermelon Pickle

Let us not forget the ways of our grandmothers: they had a lot
going for them in the kitchen! This old favorite makes a grand
appetizer when served chilled on a hot day.

 ¼ cup salt
 2 pounds watermelon rind, trimmed and diced into 1-inch
    cubes
 2 pounds sugar
 3 cups cider vinegar
 1 lemon, thinly sliced (discard seeds)
 1 inch stick cinnamon, crushed
 1 tablespoon whole cloves, crushed
 1 tablespoon whole allspice, crushed

Pour 4 cups of water into a large, enamel-lined kettle, add salt,
and stir to dissolve. Add watermelon rind, cover, and soak overnight. Drain brine and discard. Rinse the pot and add water to
cover the rind. Boil until rind is tender, about 1½ hours. Keep
rind covered with water by adding more hot water if needed.

After about 1 hour, using a separate pot, bring the sugar,
2 cups cold water, vinegar, and lemon slices to a boil. Wrap the
lightly crushed cinnamon, cloves, and allspice in cheesecloth as
a bouquet garni, and add this to pickling solution. Boil for 30
minutes. Drain the watermelon rind and add it to the pickling
solution. Lower heat and simmer, uncovered, for about 2 hours
until the rind is translucent and the syrup is rather thick. Remove bouquet garni.

Spoon the boiling hot pickles into warmed, sterile pint-size
preserving jars, leaving at least ¼ inch of space at the top. Put on
lids and seal tightly. Mature for 10 minutes by setting jars in a
boiling water bath. Cool. Store pickles on a cool, dark shelf.

MAKES ABOUT 3 PINTS

Soups

Andalusian Gazpacho

A genuine Spanish gazpacho—not as delicate as some others, but robust in a way that would satisfy a good gypsy family. The simple ingredients tell you the difference between this soup and its imitations. Use more than three cloves of garlic if you wish. The following recipe gives a chunkier version.

    3 tablespoons good heavy Spanish olive oil
    1 quart water
    3 cups cubed soft bread
    4 large ripe tomatoes, cubed
    3 cloves garlic, mashed
    3 tablespoons red wine vinegar
    salt and freshly ground black pepper
    2 ice cubes
    2 small bell peppers, finely diced
    1 medium-size tomato, finely diced
    1 cucumber, peeled, seeded, and finely diced
    3 slices Italian or French bread, toasted and cubed

In a large bowl, whisk olive oil into water, and pour the mixture over the 3 cups cubed bread. Stir in the tomato cubes and the mashed garlic, and let the mixture marinate for 2 or 3 hours.

Then press the mixture through a sieve, and add the vinegar and salt and black pepper to taste. Add the ice cubes, and refrigerate for 1 hour. Meanwhile, arrange the diced peppers, tomato, cucumber, and toasted bread cubes in separate small serving dishes. When the chilled soup is served, each guest garnishes the soup to his own taste.

SERVES 4

Crunchy Gazpacho

This is something between a salad and a soup—dandy for dog days but good any time.

> 4 large tomatoes, coarsely chopped
> 1 cucumber, peeled and thinly sliced
> 1 tablespoon minced onion
> 2 tablespoons wine vinegar
> ½ bell pepper, minced
> 2 tablespoons olive oil
> 1 clove garlic, bruised
> dash cayenne or 4 shakes Tabasco
> 4 slices lime

Combine ingredients, except for lime slices, and chill for 4 hours. Remove garlic clove. Serve over ice cubes in mugs, garnishing each with a slice of lime.

SERVES 4

❧ Bayou Bean Soup

An authentic New Orleans recipe, a rich, hearty, velvety purée. Take the time to prepare this marvel, for it deserves all your attention; results can be splendid. (Don't attempt to start it without the ham bone, though.)

> 2 pounds red beans
> 1 pound ham, cut into bite-size chunks
> 1 large ham bone
> 4 onions, chopped
> 6 whole scallions, chopped
> 4 stalks celery, chopped
> 3 tablespoons minced fresh parsley
> 3 cloves garlic, minced
> 1 fat bell pepper, chopped
> 1 teaspoon salt
> freshly ground black pepper
> dash cayenne
> dash dried red pepper flakes
> ¼ teaspoon thyme
> 2 bay leaves

Soak beans overnight in water to cover (or use the quick-soak method, p. 165). The following day, drain beans and put them in a large soup kettle with all other ingredients and 1 gallon of water. Bring to a boil, then lower heat and simmer for 4 to 5 hours. Turn off heat.

Remove ham bone and discard. Scoop out the pieces of ham with a slotted spoon and put them in a large bowl. Strain the soup through a colander into another soup pot, mashing the beans with the back of a wooden spoon. Remove about 1 cup of the mashed beans from the colander and mix them in the bowl with the ham pieces. Push the rest of the beans through the colander and return to soup kettle. Warm the soup over low heat for about 10 minutes, stirring to keep it smooth. To serve, put a bit of the mashed bean and ham mixture in each bowl and fill with the creamy soup.

SERVES 6

ℜ Chile Frijoles Soup

For this authentic, traditional Mexican dish, only frijoles, the pink Mexican beans, should be used, and only fresh chilies, not powder. You can substitute pinto beans if you must. If you cannot obtain fresh green chilies, which you can get in a Latin American market, use canned whole green chilies; however, canned chilies lack the gusto that characterizes this dish at its best.

> 1 pound frijoles
> 1 onion, coarsely chopped
> 2 cloves garlic, chopped
> 1 tablespoon oregano
> 1 fresh green chili or 2 canned chilies, mashed
> about ½ tablespoon salt
> ½ cup mild grated goat cheese (optional)
> croutons (optional)

Wash and pick over beans, and soak them overnight (or use quick-soak method, p. 165). Drain beans and put them in a large kettle with 2 quarts cold water. Bring to a boil, and simmer for at least 4 to 6 hours. If beans start to become dry, add boiling water, 1 cup at a time. When beans are tender, add the onion, garlic, oregano, and mashed chili. Simmer 15 minutes, remove from heat, and rub mixture through a colander into another pot. Reheat slowly, adding boiling water until soup is a rich purée. Add salt to taste.

If using grated goat cheese, stir it in 15 minutes before serving.

Serve with well-buttered sourdough bread, or top each bowl with croutons made by frying small cubes of dried bread in olive oil.

SERVES 4 TO 6

🎯 Black Bean Soup Supreme

The perfect recipe for leftover black beans (although it can be made from scratch, see p. 167).

2 cups cooked black beans
1 quart water
3 strips bacon, crisply fried and crumbled, or 3 tablespoons
    diced cooked ham
1½ tablespoons butter
1 onion, chopped
1 small carrot, minced
2 stalks celery, including leaves, chopped
2 tablespoons chopped fresh parsley
1 leek, halved lengthwise, or 2 whole scallions, chopped
½ teaspoon dry mustard
1 cup light cream
½ teaspoon salt
freshly ground black pepper
¼ cup dark rum
½ cup croutons
4 thin slices lemon
sprinkling Hungarian paprika

Gently mash beans with a fork in a large soup pot. (A food processor or blender will purée them too finely.) Add water and bacon or ham. Bring to a boil, and lower heat to simmer. In a skillet, melt the butter and sauté the onion, carrot, celery, parsley, and leek or scallions.

When vegetables are wilted, add to the beans. Add the mustard, cream, salt, and pepper to taste. Simmer for 15 minutes. Just before serving, stir in the rum.

Top each soup bowl with handful of croutons and 1 thin lemon slice dusted with paprika.

SERVES 4

ℵ Pinto Bean Soup

A standby of the Old West that sticks to the ribs. A cup for company, or a big bowl apiece for a hungry family of four. Crusty over-warmed bread is a must with this.

1 pound pinto beans
2 tablespoons lard or oil
2 pounds meaty beef bones
3 quarts water
1 large onion, sliced
2 cloves garlic, mashed
6 peppercorns, cracked
2 teaspoons salt
½ teaspoon powdered cumin, or 1 teaspoon cumin seed
½ teaspoon crushed coriander seed
1 small dried red pepper, seeded and minced
2 bay leaves

Soak pinto beans overnight or use quick-soak method (p. 165).

In a large soup pot, heat lard or oil over high flame, and brown beef bones quickly. Drain beans and add them; then add all other ingredients. Bring to a boil, lower heat, and simmer, covered, for about 2 hours, until meat and beans are tender. Discard bay leaves. Remove meat, cut in small pieces, and discard bones. Return meat to pot and serve.

SERVES 4 FOR A MEAL,
8 TO 10 AS A FIRST COURSE

Callalou

Also spelled *callilu, callau,* or *callaloo,* all of which refer to a kind of soup much favored in the West Indies—one that features the chardlike green leaves of the callalou plant. Some claim the callalou leaves are really from two separate plants: the taro and the Chinese spinach. Either Swiss chard or fresh spinach will do nicely as a substitute. The soup itself ranges from utter simplicity to a grand elaboration. Here, in summary, is a simple version from Martinique.

In a big soup pot half filled with water, boil a good piece of ham or a ham bone.

Add chopped callalou greens, okras, scallions, a bouquet garni, salt and pepper, and fresh hot red pepper, chopped. Simmer about an hour. Serve with rice as a side dish, or with grilled salt codfish.

And here is a more specific version:

    1 ham bone
    1 package fresh spinach, or 1 bunch Swiss chard
        (about ¾ pound), washed and chopped
    4 okra pods, chopped
    4 cloves garlic, chopped
    4 whole scallions, chopped
    2 tiny carrots, chopped
    1 fresh hot red pepper, seeded and minced
    about 3 quarts water
    1 tablespoon minced fresh parsley

Follow directions above.

SERVES 4

♋ Delta Gumbo

In the Delta region, there are as many versions of gumbo as there
are crawdaddies. If you can find the filé powder and the okra,
you'll have no problem with this recipe; and you'll have a guest-
pleasing winner. Plan to make this when you have amounts of
leftover cooked meats too small to do anything else with. Filé
is the powdered young leaves of the sassafras plant. It can be
obtained by mail order (see Mail-Order Sources).

> 2 tablespoons bacon fat
> 1 onion, minced
> 4 stalks celery, minced
> ¼ bell pepper, minced
> 1 teaspoon grated lemon peel
> 1 bay leaf
> 3 tablespoons minced fresh parsley
> 4 large tomatoes, peeled and coarsely chopped
> 1 clove garlic, minced
> ¼ teaspoon powdered cumin
> ½ teaspoon salt
> freshly ground black pepper
> 6 cups chicken stock
> 1 cup fresh corn kernels, or 10-ounce package frozen corn
> 10-ounce package frozen okra, thawed and finely sliced
> any leftover cooked chicken, ham, and/or sausage,
>   cut into small pieces
> ½ teaspoon filé powder
> 3 slices bacon, well cooked and crumbled

Heat bacon fat in a large, heavy pot, and brown the onion, celery,
and bell pepper. Add lemon peel, bay leaf, parsley, tomatoes,
garlic, cumin, salt, a generous grinding of pepper, and stock.
Cover and bring to a boil, then lower heat and simmer for 10
minutes. Add corn and okra and cook over high heat for 8 minutes, stirring frequently. Add chicken and any other meats, stir
again, and correct seasoning. Stir in filé powder just before serving. Serve in soup plates, with a sprinkling of bacon bits.

SERVES 6 TO 8

℘ Gombo aux Herbes
Delta Gumbo with Herbs

Gumbos are as varied as Louisiana ethnic types. This version is more sophisticated than most; perhaps it speaks with a French accent. The culinary accent is on fresh greens—whatever your palate fancies.

1 young cabbage, cored and coarsely chopped
1 pound spinach, coarsely chopped
1 handful greens such as turnip tops or radish tops, chopped
1 bunch watercress, chopped
1 bunch fresh parsley, chopped
2 pounds brisket of veal, boned
¾ pound lean ham
2 tablespoons butter
1 onion, chopped
¼ teaspoon marjoram
¼ teaspoon thyme
1 bay leaf
½ dried red pepper, seeded and minced
3 whole cloves
¼ teaspoon powdered allspice
½ teaspoon salt
freshly ground black pepper to taste
3 cups cooked long-grain rice

Parboil the chopped cabbage and spinach in a large iron pot, in 4 quarts of water. Add turnip tops or radish tops. Add the watercress and parsley. After 5 minutes, drain vegetables and save liquid. Finely chop vegetables.

Trim fat from the veal and ham, and cut into 1-inch slices. Brown in iron skillet in hot butter, adding chopped onion after 3 minutes. When onion begins to turn golden, lower heat. Add the chopped greens and stir-fry until well browned. Bring greens water to boil, and add the meat and greens. There should be about 3 quarts of liquid. Next, add all the seasonings. Bring to a boil, lower heat, and simmer for 1 hour. Serve with rice.

SERVES 6 TO 8

ℵ Chinese Pork and Cucumber Soup

A delicate soup with a surprising range of flavors.

    1 pound roast pork shoulder, julienned
    4 scallions, sliced into 1-inch pieces
    4 cups chicken broth
    4 teaspoons soy sauce
    ½ teaspoon Chinese hot oil or Tabasco
    3 cucumbers

Put julienned pork (sliced 2 inches long, ⅛ inch wide and thick), scallions, broth, soy sauce, and Chinese hot oil or Tabasco in a soup pot and bring to a boil. Simmer for 5 minutes. While soup cooks, peel the cucumbers. Slice each in half lengthwise, remove seeds, and julienne, about the same size as the pork shreds. Add to the soup and simmer 4 minutes more, until cucumber turns transparent. Serve immediately.

SERVES 4 TO 6

ℵ Gulyas Soup

This is indeed a soup, but what a soup! If you serve it as a first course instead of as a main dish, it can only be because you are having either Stendahl or Gargantua as a guest.

    3 onions, chopped
    2 tablespoons butter
    1½ pounds soup beef, cubed
    2 tablespoons Hungarian paprika
    1 quart strong beef broth
    1 clove garlic, mashed
    ¼ teaspoon marjoram
    ¼ teaspoon caraway seed
    ½ teaspoon minced lemon peel
    1 medium potato, peeled and diced
    salt

In a soup pot, sauté the chopped onions in butter until golden. Add the meat and the paprika and brown meat slightly. Add the broth, garlic, marjoram, caraway, and lemon peel. Simmer for 1½ hours, partly covered. Add potato dice and simmer 30 minutes longer. Salt to taste.

SERVES 3 AS A MAIN DISH

🎋 Hot-and-Sour Soup

This classic Chinese soup deserves the popularity it has enjoyed for centuries. All the exotic ingredients are available in Chinese markets or may be ordered (see Mail-Order Sources).

3 or 4 dried black mushrooms (shiitake)
1 cup warm water
1 tablespoon cornstarch
¼ cup water
5 cups chicken stock
¼ pound cooked lean pork, shredded
½ cup canned bamboo shoots, shredded
¼ cup lily buds, cut in half
2 cakes bean curd, thinly sliced
1 tablespoon dry sherry
2 tablespoons rice vinegar or white vinegar
2 teaspoons soy sauce
½ teaspoon Chinese hot oil
1 egg, beaten
few drops Chinese sesame oil
1 whole scallion, minced

Clean dried mushrooms by rinsing, then soak in 1 cup warm water for 20 minutes. Reserve liquid. Slice mushrooms into thin strips, discarding stems. Blend cornstarch in ¼ cup water to make a smooth paste. Put stock and mushroom liquid (discard any residue) in a soup pot and bring to a boil. Add pork, bamboo shoots, mushroom strips, and lily buds. Cover and simmer for 10 minutes. Add bean curd, cover, and simmer 3 minutes more. Stir in sherry, vinegar, soy sauce, and hot oil. Thicken slightly with a little of the cornstarch paste. Slowly add beaten egg, stirring gently. Immediately remove from heat. Dot surface with a few drops of sesame oil and top with minced scallion.

SERVES 6

🎵 La Soupe z'Habitants from Martinique

A typical Antilles special, the proportions and ingredients of which vary with each household. If you are in doubt, measure ingredients similar to your own favorite vegetable soup. The spelling seems to be in Martinique dialect, derived from the "native soup" so beloved by French-Canadians.

cabbage
spinach
leeks
carrots
celery
squash
green beans
onions
any other fresh greens
1 or 2 tablespoons oil
1 ham hock or beef knuckle
salt and freshly ground black pepper
1 fresh green chili, minced

Cut up into small pieces: cabbage, spinach, leeks, carrots, celery, squash, green beans, onions, and any other fresh greens.

Fry the vegetables in a bit of oil in a big iron pot. Throw in a ham hock or a beef knuckle, and add water to cover. Stir occasionally with a lele (a forked twig, used like a wooden spoon), and simmer partly covered about 1 hour. During last 10 minutes season with salt, pepper, and minced chili.

SERVES AS MANY AS NECESSARY

♋ Mulligatawny

This soup has nothing to do with mulligan stew, and it isn't Irish.
It is a dish from southern India, and the name comes from two
Tamil words: *molegoo* (pepper) and *tunnee* (water). Pepper-
water comes in many variations; here are two authentic versions.

Mulligatawny I

12 peppercorns
2 cloves garlic
2 rounded tablespoons coriander seed
1 tablespoon cumin seed
1 tablespoon fenugreek seed
1 rounded teaspoon mustard seed
1 quart rich meat or vegetable stock

Put the spices into a muslin or cheesecloth bag, and simmer for
30 minutes in the stock. Discard spice bag and serve broth.

SERVES 6

Mulligatawny II

This version is meatier in all ways.

2 large onions
6 tablespoons butter
1 clove garlic, mashed
1 teaspoon turmeric
1 teaspoon dried red pepper flakes
1 teaspoon cumin seed
½ teaspoon powdered coriander
½ teaspoon powdered ginger
1 frying chicken, cut into 8 pieces
1 teaspoon poppy seed, ground
1 quart rich beef or other meat stock
salt
3 lemons, cut in wedges

Finely slice the onions. Set one aside for later. In a large, lidded
skillet, melt the butter until sizzling, and add 1 sliced onion,

garlic, turmeric, dried red pepper flakes, cumin, coriander, and ginger. After 5 minutes of stirring, add the chicken pieces. When chicken is golden brown (about 5 minutes more), add poppy seed, stock, and salt to taste. Sauté the second sliced onion separately and then put it over the chicken. Cover tightly and simmer for about 35 minutes, or until chicken is tender. Serve a lemon wedge with each steaming bowl, so that the lemon may be squeezed into the soup just before eating.

SERVES 6 TO 8

🎜 Old-Time Dark Beer Soup

This is not so much spicy as it is amazing. The chillier the weather, the better the taste.

½ loaf dry whole-wheat bread
36 ounces (3 bottles) dark beer
½ cup maple syrup
dash powdered ginger
pinch each salt, freshly ground black pepper, and
    caraway seed

Crumble bread and soak well in 1 bottle (12 ounces) of beer. Put through coarse sieve. Heat remainder of beer in pan with all the other ingredients, add the sieved bread, and mix thoroughly. Reheat to boiling over low fire, stirring often. Serve at once.

SERVES 4

🎜 Philadelphia Pepper Pot

Legend has it that this All-American dish was invented during the bitter winter of 1777, when George Washington's ragged army was near starvation at Valley Forge. With the larder almost empty, the General ordered his chef to come up with some hearty nourishment. Foraging provided odds and ends that made for a sturdy soup-stew. The dish so heartened the men that General

Washington, it is said, named it after his cook's hometown. Legend or no, it is a fact that Philadelphia pepper pot is one of the few really spicy native American classics.

Some non-Philadelphians like to top the broth with Hungarian-Style Little Dumplings (p. 257).

> 2 pounds tripe
> 1 veal knuckle with meat left on
> 2 pounds marrow bones, cracked by butcher
> 2 large onions, diced
> 1 bay leaf
> 1 carrot, diced
> ½ teaspoon thyme
> ½ teaspoon dried red pepper flakes
> 1 teaspoon powdered allspice
> 6 whole cloves
> 4 potatoes, finely diced
> salt and freshly ground black pepper
> 2 tablespoons chopped fresh parsley

Wash tripe and put it into a large kettle with 1 gallon of water. Bring to a boil, then cover and reduce heat. Cook over low flame for 6 hours, or until tripe is tender. Let cool, pour broth into a container, and refrigerate. Slice the tripe into very small pieces, and refrigerate.

While tripe is simmering, put the veal knuckle into a second kettle with 2 quarts of water, and set over low heat. Add the marrow bones to the veal pot. Add the onions, bay leaf, carrot, thyme, dried red pepper flakes, allspice, and cloves. Simmer this mixture, partly covered, for about 5 hours. Cool veal broth until meat can be handled easily, and cut the veal into very small pieces. Discard bones and refrigerate the veal with the tripe. Pour broth through a sieve into container with the tripe broth. Refrigerate for several hours or overnight, until the fat congeals on the broth. Skim off fat and discard. In a large kettle combine broth with the tripe and veal. Simmer over low heat for about 30 minutes. Add the diced potatoes, simmer for 15 minutes more, and season to taste. Just before serving, sprinkle the soup with the parsley.

SERVES 6 TO 8

🎵 Senegalese Soup

Dakar is the exotic capital of Senegal, a slice of West Africa
heavily under French influence, especially in the kitchen. I've
had both delicious native food and rather splendid French meals
in Dakar. I suspect Senegalese soup is a made-up concoction
rather than an authentic dish. There are many versions (which
tends to support my theory), and this one is among the best.
With its chutney and curry powder, I should think a more apt
name for this offering might be Bengalese soup. This soup is
fine served hot, also perfect served chilled in the summertime.

> 2 tablespoons butter
> 1 tablespoon curry powder (p. 13)
> 2 tablespoons flour
> 2 cups heated chicken broth
> 1 cup julienned cooked chicken, preferably breast
> 2 tablespoons minced chutney (Major Grey–type
>   suggested)
> 2 egg yolks
> ½ cup heavy cream
> 4 teaspoons minced fresh chives

In a heavy saucepan, melt butter over moderate heat and blend
in curry powder. Cook and stir a minute to take away the raw
taste of the curry, then add the flour and stir to make a roux. Let
it bubble gently for about 1 minute. Add hot broth all at once, stir
vigorously, and increase heat until the mixture commences to
boil. Reduce heat immediately and add the chicken and chutney.
Simmer for 10 minutes to blend flavors.

Meanwhile, beat egg yolks in a separate bowl and add
cream, beating well. Set saucepan over lowest heat, and add 2
spoonfuls of the hot mixture to the yolks. Stir well, then pour
yolks into the saucepan. Stir constantly for a minute or two—
be sure not to boil the soup. Ladle into individual bowls, top with
chives, and serve.

SERVES 4

𝕊𝕃 Red Pepper Jellied Consommé

Not all hot soups have to be hot. I say this to underline the impoverishment of the English language, which has no satisfactory distinction between "heat-hot" and "spice-hot." This, at any rate, is a chilled, spicy soup.

    4 ounces pimiento
    1 quart rich chicken stock
    ½ cup dry sherry
    ½ teaspoon cayenne
    2 tablespoons chopped fresh chives

Purée the pimiento in a blender. Add a bit of stock, blend, and pour purée into a tureen. Add the rest of the stock, the sherry, and cayenne. Mix well, and chill for at least 1 hour before serving. Top each individual bowl of consommé with a sprinkling of the chives.

SERVES 4

𝕊𝕃 Onion Soup

French cooks can given you an argument over the differences between *soupe à l'oignon* and *gratinée* until the cheese freezes over. Stock or water—or milk—in the base? Chicken stock, veal, or beef? Gruyère, Roquefort, Camembert, or Brie? Bind the soup with egg yolks or just slosh some good Cognac in it? To strain or not to strain? We keep it very simple, but we keep it very good. Remember, a good onion soup never starts with a can of bouillon.

    2 large yellow onions, sliced paper thin
    2 tablespoons butter
    1 quart hearty homemade stock, preferably beef
    generous grinding black pepper
    ¼ cup Cognac or brandy (optional)
    4 slices French bread, preferably sourdough,
        toasted (optional)
    ⅔ cup grated genuine Swiss or French Gruyère (optional)

In a heavy saucepan, sauté onions until golden—do not let them scorch. Add the broth and the pepper, cover, and simmer until the onions are tender, at least 30 minutes. Just before serving, add the brandy.

If you want the onion soup gratinéed, preheat oven to 400° F. When the soup is done, ladle it into four to six oven-proof bowls and float a toasted round on top. Sprinkle cheese to entirely cover the top of each bowl. Bake until cheese is melted and lightly brown.

SERVES 4 TO 6

 ## Sopa de Ajo
Spanish Garlic Soup

This is not quite as powerful as it sounds. As the garlic starts hopping around in the hot oil it loses some of its primordial ardor.

> 2 tablespoons olive oil, the finer the better
> 6 slices coarse white bread, finely diced
> 10 cloves garlic, split in half
> 3 tablespoons minced fresh parsley
> 1 cup tomato juice
> 5 cups chicken stock
> 4 eggs

Heat olive oil in a deep kettle, add diced bread and garlic, and stir over medium heat until golden. Don't burn! Remove with slotted spoon and mash in mortar and pestle. Work in the parsley, then add the tomato juice. Return mixture to kettle, and add the stock. Bring to a boil, lower heat, and simmer 10 minutes. Break the eggs gently into the simmering liquid, cover, and poach until the whites are just set. Serve one egg, with soup, in each bowl.

SERVES 4

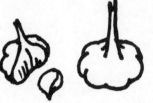

ℜ Tourain à l'Ail
Iced Garlic Soup

A variation on the garlic soup theme, with rather more of a French accent than usual. It probably originated in Provence, although the use of nutmeg in that region is unexpected. But—*iced?* What a novelty!

Thinly sliced French bread or Melba toast makes an excellent accompaniment.

1 teaspoon salt
12 cloves garlic
2 tablespoons olive oil
1 tablespoon butter
4 cups strong chicken stock
¼ teaspoon dried red pepper flakes
salt and freshly ground black pepper
3 egg yolks
1 cup heavy cream
grating fresh nutmeg
2 teaspoons minced fresh chives

Pour the salt onto a plate and chop the garlic into it (this method saves all the garlic oil and makes the garlic easy to handle). In the bottom of a heavy soup pot, heat the oil and butter. Add the garlic and salt, and sauté lightly until the garlic is golden brown. Add chicken stock, dried red peppers, and salt and pepper to taste. Bring to a boil slowly, lower heat, and simmer for 30 minutes.

In a large bowl, beat the egg yolks thoroughly. Little by little, strain the soup through cheesecloth onto the beaten yolks, stirring constantly so the eggs don't curdle. Return the mixture to the soup pot, and stir over low heat until soup thickens. Do not boil. Remove from heat, and chill for at least 1 hour. Stir in the cream. Serve in small bowls, preferably over cracked ice, sprinkling the top of each bowl with nutmeg and chives.

SERVES 6 TO 8

Borani
Yogurt Soup

In the summertime, when you serve a good curry dinner, this makes a spicy yet cooling appetizer.

> 2 cups yogurt
> 1 quart cold water
> ½ teaspoon chopped fresh mint, or ¼ teaspoon dried
> ¼ teaspoon chili powder
> dash salt
> freshly ground black pepper to taste
> 4 ice cubes, cracked
> 8 to 10 strips lemon peel

Put all ingredients except lemon peel in a cocktail shaker and shake well, or put in a bowl and whisk. When thoroughly blended, pour in soup bowls, and garnish with lemon peel.

SERVES 8 TO 10

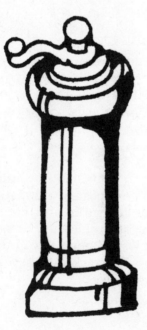

Sopa de Albóndigas
Mexican Meatball Soup

The real thing from the Old Southwest. Typical of such honest peasant dishes, it is easy to make, it's filling, and it has a magnificent aroma.

Albondigas
1 pound ground beef
½ pound ground pork
1 slice bread
1 cup water
1 egg
1 onion, minced
1 clove garlic, chopped
1 teaspoon minced cilantro (fresh coriander)
1 teaspoon salt
pinch oregano
pinch dried mint leaves
freshly ground black pepper
2 tablespoons lard or vegetable oil

Grind beef and pork together. Soak bread in the water, and squeeze dry. Discard water. Mix bread with the meat. Add egg, onion, and all seasonings. Blend thoroughly with your hands, and form walnut-size meatballs. Heat lard or oil in a skillet over high flame, and brown albondigas on all sides. Set them aside.

Stock
35-ounce can tomatoes
½ cup fresh green chili pulp or 2 rounded tablespoons authentic chili powder
1 teaspoon salt
1 teaspoon oregano

Rub the tomatoes through a colander into a soup pot. Add enough water to make 2 quarts of liquid, and bring to a boil. Add the chili pulp or powder, salt, and oregano. Boil down to 3 pints of liquid. Turn to simmer, and add the albondigas by lowering them gently into the broth with a spoon. Simmer for 20 minutes.

SERVES 4 TO 6

🎵 Yuk Chai Chang
Korean Hot Spice Soup

There are half a dozen Korean restaurants in New York, and it has always amazed me that Americans haven't literally gobbled up Korean cuisine, for it is based almost entirely on beef. Not listed on any menu, but apparently always in the kitchen for the cognoscenti, is a frankly fiery soup that is a delicious concoction. Ask your waiter, phonetically, for "yook jay jang"; literally, "Tear beef to pieces hot spice in soup!" This may get results if "yuk chai chang" does not.

This is a royal potage that almost rivals the heavenly hot-and-sour soup of China. Yet it has its own character. Failing to surmount language barriers, in desperation I finally concocted my own version.

On authenticity: For the real thing, you simmer shortribs to make the stock, and fine-shred the meat into the soup. My way works fine, and saves time. "Rice sticks" are cellophane noodles, and authentic; Chinese egg noodles are a passable substitute.

> 1 tablespoon peanut oil
> 1 large onion, minced
> 2 cloves garlic, minced
> 1 stalk celery, finely sliced
> ¼ pound lean ground beef
> 1 leaf celery cabbage or lettuce, shredded
> 3 quarter-size slices fresh ginger, minced
> 4 cups rich beef stock
> 3 tablespoons fresh peas
> 1 whole scallion, cut into ½-inch slices
> ½ teaspoon sesame seed
> 1 handful rice sticks or Chinese egg noodles
> dash sesame oil
> 2 sprigs cilantro (fresh coriander), chopped
> 1 egg, beaten

Heat peanut oil over highest flame in wok or deep cast-iron pot. When oil is sizzling hot, add onion, garlic, celery, and ground beef, breaking beef into small bits as you add it. Stir-fry over high heat until meat loses redness—about 5 minutes. Add shredded cabbage or lettuce and ginger. Stir. Turn heat to medium and add stock. Bring to a boil, turn heat to low, and stir in peas, scallion, and sesame seed. Quickly add the rice sticks or noodles, raise heat, and boil until they are barely done (test by biting). Add sesame oil and cilantro, and stir again. Add beaten egg and stir quickly to mix everything. Serve at once.

SERVES 6 AS A FIRST COURSE,
OR 2 AS A MAIN DISH, WITH
ADDITIONAL NOODLES

🎗 Spanish Cabbage Soup

This came my way as a soup ostensibly originating in Galicia, Spain. It seems decidedly Mexican to me. Perhaps the cabbage makes it Iberian.

¼ cup olive oil
1 pound beef chuck, cut into ½-inch cubes
1 large onion, chopped
3 cloves garlic, finely chopped
1 bell pepper, finely chopped
2 dried red peppers, seeded and minced, or
    1 teaspoon dried red pepper flakes
1 cup dried chickpeas, soaked overnight, or use quick-soak
    method (p. 165)
2 quarts water
1 tablespoon salt
½ teaspoon cumin seed, crushed
1 small cabbage, cored and shredded

In a heavy kettle, heat oil over high flame, and sauté the beef until it loses its redness. Lower the flame to moderate, add the onion, garlic, and peppers, and stir until the onions are transparent (about 5 minutes). Drain the chickpeas and add them to the kettle. Add the water, salt, and cumin seed. Bring to a boil, then turn to simmer, cover, and cook gently for 2 hours, until chickpeas are tender. Add cabbage, cover again, and cook just 15 minutes. The cabbage should remain crisp.

SERVES 6

✿ Soupe au Vin
Wine Soup

A tangy soup, wonderful to return to after a brisk winter walk.

    12 whole cloves
    12 allspice berries
    2 sticks cinnamon
    2 quarts good chicken stock
    1 cup port or Madeira

Tie spices in muslin bag and heat slowly to boiling point in the stock. Simmer for 20 minutes. When the soup is ready, remove spices and pour liquid into a tureen. Add the wine and serve.

SERVES 8

Seafood & Fish

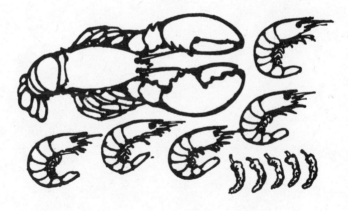

🎵 Shrimp and Tomato, Bahia-Style

Bahia is that edge of Brazil still yearning toward Africa, the closest point to the continent from which most of the Bahaians come. A tinge of Spanish, a strong dash of African, and you get a spicy dish that doesn't fool around. For this typical tingler, if you do not care for shrimp, substitute fish fillets or even chicken.

    1 cup grated unsweetened coconut
    1 cup milk
    3 tablespoons oil
    1 onion, finely chopped
    5 tomatoes, peeled, seeded, and chopped
    handful fresh parsley, chopped
    2 pounds shrimp, shelled and deveined
    ½ teaspoon salt
    freshly ground black pepper to taste
    1 tablespoon butter
    1 tablespoon flour
    2 small dried red peppers, seeded and minced
    2 cups cooked long-grain rice

Make coconut milk according to recipe on p. 222.

In a large saucepan, heat the oil and sauté the onion until it is translucent. Add the tomatoes and parsley, and sauté 3 minutes longer. Add the shrimp, salt, and pepper, stirring constantly for 3 minutes. Remove from heat.

In a second small saucepan, over low heat, melt the butter, add flour, and stir to make a roux, about 1 minute. Add coconut milk slowly, stirring all the while, until slightly thickened. Add this sauce to the shrimp mixture and stir in the peppers. Simmer for 3 minutes. Transfer to a warm platter and serve surrounded by rice.

SERVES 4

⚘ Shrimp with Mustard Fruits, Four Seasons

A splendid dish from one of New York's premier restaurants. Mustard fruits may be obtained at gourmet delicatessens and other specialty food stores or from Mail-Order Sources (p. 289).

2½ pounds large shrimp
4 cups court bouillon (following recipe)
1 cup mustard fruits, with liquid

Batter
4 cups flour
2 tablespoons vegetable oil
1 teaspoon baking powder
3 cups water
2 egg yolks
salt to taste
flour for dipping

Sauce
2 cups béchamel sauce (p. 221)
2 tablespoons dry mustard
¼ cup mustard fruits in chunks
4 tablespoons deep-fried fresh parsley (optional)

Poach shrimp in court bouillon until they turn pink, about 4 minutes. Drain. Shell and devein.

Mince the cup of mustard fruits in their liquid. Split shrimp halfway through and stuff with the minced fruits. Pat firmly so that stuffing remains in shrimp.

Make a thick batter by mixing flour, oil, baking powder, water, egg yolks, and salt. (This may be prepared in advance and refrigerated.) Roll shrimp in flour, dip into batter, and deep-fry at 400° F. in oil for 4 to 6 minutes, until brown. Drain.

Mix béchamel with the dry mustard and the ¼ cup mustard fruits. Heat until piping hot. Serve in a separate dish as a sauce for the shrimp.

Deep-fried parsley makes an attractive garnish for the shrimp.

SERVES 6 AS AN APPETIZER,
4 AS A MAIN COURSE

Court Bouillon
Wine Sauce for Cooking Fish

There are many recipes for court bouillon. This is one of the simplest, and it works well. It is especially suited to cooking shellfish.

For Shrimp with Mustard Fruits, Four Seasons (preceding recipe), use half this recipe.

½ pound fish bones, heads, and trims
1 quart water
1 bottle dry white wine
1 large onion, stuck with 3 cloves
2 bay leaves
2 cloves garlic
1 teaspoon thyme
1 teaspoon salt
6 peppercorns, bruised

Place fish scraps in the water, cover, and simmer for 15 minutes. Strain well and discard scraps. Rinse out pan and add the strained broth and the rest of the ingredients. Simmer, uncovered, for 20 minutes and strain once more.

MAKES ABOUT 2 QUARTS

✿ Creole Seafood Gumbo

Many think a gumbo is not one if it lacks okra or filé powder to thicken it. So here is a gumbo with okra.

1½ pounds smoked sausage, thinly sliced
¾ pound boiled ham, diced
4 tablespoons flour
2 onions, finely chopped
4 to 6 whole scallions, finely chopped
2 stalks celery, finely chopped
1 large bell pepper, finely chopped
2 sprigs fresh parsley, minced
4 cloves garlic, minced
3 pounds shrimp, cleaned and deveined
4 quarts water
1 bay leaf
1 teaspoon thyme
35-ounce can tomatoes
1 pound fresh okra, sliced, or 10-ounce package frozen
2 teaspoons salt
freshly ground black pepper
½ teaspoon dried red pepper flakes
½ pound crabmeat
12 oysters and their liquor
6 cups cooked long-grain rice

In a large iron soup pot, brown the sausages over low heat, using no fat. Remove sausages and pour off all but ¼ cup drippings. Brown diced ham lightly in drippings, and remove. Stir the flour into drippings and make a roux, browning gently over low heat—it may take 15 minutes to do this properly. Add onions, scallions, celery, bell pepper, parsley, and garlic. Cook over low heat, stirring frequently until soft—about 10 minutes.

Add shrimp and cook and stir until they turn orange-red. Return sausage and ham to pot and slowly add the water. Add bay leaf and thyme. Mash tomatoes with wooden spoon and add them to the pot. When water begins to boil, add okra, salt, a generous grinding of black pepper, and the red pepper flakes.

Cover and simmer 45 minutes. Skim off foam if any accumulates. Add crabmeat, oysters, and oyster liquor. Simmer 10 minutes.

Gumbo may be served as soon as it is cooked. However, it is better if cooked early, refrigerated several hours, and then reheated. Serve with rice.

SERVES 12

‰ Kan-Shoa Ming-Hsia
Prawns in the Szechuan Manner

Madame Cecilia Chiang, a great lady from Peking, owns two West Coast restaurants of renown, both named the Mandarin. One Mandarin graces the famous Ghiradelli Square in San Francisco; the other is located in Beverly Hills. Madame Chiang is credited with being the first to introduce authentic Northern Chinese cuisine to the West Coast. We are grateful for her special version of a classic Szechuan dish.

    1 tablespoon cornstarch
    2 tablespoons water
    2 tablespoons peanut oil
    8 prawns or jumbo shrimp, shelled and deveined
    1 clove garlic, minced
    ½ teaspoon grated fresh ginger
    1 whole scallion, chopped
    1 teaspoon seeded and finely chopped dried red peppers
    2 tablespoons dry sherry
    1 tablespoon catsup
    tiny pinch of sugar
    sesame oil

Mix cornstarch and water together; set aside. Set a wok over high heat. When it is very hot, dribble the peanut oil along the inside rim. Add prawns or shrimp, garlic, ginger, scallion, and red peppers. Toss and stir about 1 minute. Add sherry, catsup, and sugar. Add cornstarch mixture. Continue to toss and stir until mixture thickens and the prawns are cooked, about 3 to 4 minutes, depending on their size. Just before serving, dot lightly with sesame oil.

SERVES 2 AS A MAIN DISH

🙦 Trinidad Shrimp Curry

From the land of calypso, a different kind of curry. Serve it with boiled rice and your favorite chutneys.

    1½ teaspoons coriander seed
    1½ teaspoons cumin seed
    1½ teaspoons mustard seed
    1 tablespoon black peppercorns
    ½ teaspoon dried red pepper flakes
    2 bay leaves
    3 tablespoons oil
    3 tablespoons sweet butter
    2 large onions, finely chopped
    2 cloves garlic, mashed
    1 tablespoon minced fresh ginger
    4 tomatoes, chopped
    2 tablespoons lime juice
    ½ cup water or chicken stock, if needed
    2 pounds jumbo shrimp, shelled and deveined
    ½ teaspoon salt

In a mortar or a blender, pulverize the coriander, cumin, and mustard seed, the peppercorns, pepper flakes, and bay leaves. Heat the oil and butter over a medium flame in a heavy skillet, and sauté onions until golden. Add garlic, ginger, and the pulverized spices, and stir for 3 minutes. Add the tomatoes and the lime juice. Cover and simmer for 30 minutes, stirring occasionally. If mixture becomes very dry, add ½ cup of water or stock, although the sauce should be thick. Add the shrimp and salt. Simmer, covered, until shrimp are firm and pink, about 5 minutes. Do not overcook.

SERVES 6

❧ Lobster Aromatic, Four Seasons

The Four Seasons Restaurant in Manhattan is one of the world's great restaurants. This dish is prepared and served tableside, and it will make a spectacular addition to your chafing dish cookery.

The velouté
6 tablespoons butter (no substitutions!)
6 tablespoons flour
2 cups hot court bouillon (p. 65)
¼ teaspoon salt
pinch white pepper

The lobster sauce
1 cup dry white wine
2 tablespoons butter
1 tablespoon anchovy paste
⅓ cup minced cooked lobster meat
dash cayenne

6 tablespoons butter
2 tablespoons chopped shallots
4½ cups sliced cooked lobster meat
¼ cup Pernod
1½ teaspoons salt
¼ teaspoon dry mustard
¼ teaspoon Hungarian paprika
¼ teaspoon cayenne
¼ teaspoon curry powder (p. 13)
squeeze of lemon juice
1 tablespoon minced fresh chives
1 tablespoon minced fresh parsley
½ cup heavy cream, whipped

First make the velouté. Melt the butter over moderate heat; stir in the flour and let roux bubble gently for about 2 minutes; be careful not to discolor by overcooking. Pour in the court bouillon and whisk constantly until mixture becomes thick and smooth. Add seasonings, reduce heat, and simmer, uncovered, for 20 minutes. Skim surface and stir from time to time. Strain through a fine sieve or cheesecloth. You will have about 1½ cups of velouté.

Now complete the lobster sauce. Put velouté in a saucepan and add the white wine. Simmer, uncovered, until sauce is reduced to about 2 cups. Beat in, 1 tablespoon at a time, the butter and the anchovy paste. Add the cooked lobster meat and the cayenne. You will have about 2 cups of sauce. Cover saucepan while you finish the dish.

Heat butter in a pan. Add shallots and sauté until soft, but do not brown. Add lobster, mix well, and allow to heat through. Gently warm Pernod, light with a match, and pour over lobster. Set aside to keep warm.

Mix salt, mustard, paprika, cayenne, and curry powder in separate bowl. Add to pan and mix well. Add lemon juice (in order to avoid having it spatter, stick a fork into the lemon meat and squeeze). Add chives, parsley, and lobster sauce and mix well. Boil rapidly 3 to 5 minutes over high fire to reduce. Remove from heat and add whipped cream, mixing well. Serve at once.

SERVES 4 TO 6

🎜 Trinidad Steamed Fish

This is a good and easy-to-make dish to serve when you want to spend your time with your guests and not in the kitchen—as long as you plan in advance to marinate the fish.

> 1 cup yogurt
> 1 dried red pepper, seeded and minced
> 1 teaspoon grated fresh ginger
> 1 bay leaf
> 2 whole cloves
> ½ teaspoon powdered cinnamon
> tiny sprinkling sugar
> 1 tablespoon melted butter
> 1½ pounds white fish fillets, such as sole or flounder

Mix all ingredients except fillets. Pour over the fish and marinate at least 6 hours, turning occasionally. Discard marinade and steam fish over boiling water, covered, for 10 minutes, or until tender.

SERVES 4

❧ Roasted or Barbecued Fish with Coconut Lemon Sauce

A fine California cook, Rickey Austin, says he was served this unusual fish dish many times in Tehuantepec, Mexico. "Always, before eating, I was given a small glass of tequila or mescal, which was to be drunk in one gulp; then, before the reaction set in, I filled my mouth with the fish. A tot of ice-cold gin or vodka would do." The dish should be hot but not fiery.

2 ripe tomatoes, coarsely diced
1 small onion, minced
1 clove garlic, minced
2 teaspoons fresh lemon juice
dash salt and freshly ground black pepper
2 fresh hot yellow peppers about 1 inch long (or 3
    canned jalapeño peppers), seeded and finely chopped
1 large white fish, or 2 small ones, 3 to 4 pounds in all
½ teaspoon olive oil
1 tablespoon olive oil (if barbecuing)
1 teaspoon coarse salt (rock or kosher)
1 cup grated fresh coconut
milk of 1 coconut
4 lettuce leaves, finely chopped
1 large cup minced cilantro (fresh coriander)

In a skillet over medium flame combine tomatoes with onion, garlic, 1 teaspoon lemon juice, dash of salt and black pepper, and the hot peppers. Cook slowly until mixture becomes a thick paste. Rub the inside of the fish with the paste, and the outside with ½ teaspoon of the olive oil.

If fish is to be roasted: wrap tightly in aluminum foil and bake in a 325° F. oven about 15 minutes, or until it flakes when pierced with a fork. Watch fish carefully; it must not disintegrate.

To barbecue: tie the fish together with string, oil the surface, and cook until brown and the flesh flakes easily, turning once. Baste often while barbecuing with the extra mixture of 1 tablespoon olive oil and 1 tablespoon lime juice, to keep fish moist.

After fish is cooked, remove to a hot platter and dust lightly with the coarse salt. Pour the shredded coconut and the coconut milk over the fish. Squirt 1 teaspoon lemon juice over all. Sprinkle finely chopped lettuce on top and any leftover tomato sauce, and serve immediately. A bowl of freshly minced cilantro should be offered so guests can top their dishes as they prefer.

SERVES 4 TO 6

Escabeche
Portuguese Pickled Fish

Escabeche in Portugal or *cebiche* in Mexico, it's a similar fishy delight in any language. In Mexico, the fish is served raw; this recipe calls for canned sardines, and it is spicier than the Mexican version.

2 cans boneless sardines in oil, preferably Portuguese
1 large onion, thinly sliced
¼ cup fine olive oil
¼ cup white vinegar
2 tablespoons minced cilantro (fresh coriander) or flat-
    leaf parsley
1 bay leaf
6 peppercorns
dash Tabasco
3 slices lemon
¼ cup water
¼ teaspoon salt
2 hard-boiled egg yolks, grated
2 ounces pimiento strips

Drain sardines and put them in a bowl. In a saucepan, combine all other ingredients except the egg yolks and pimiento. Heat to a boil, stirring occasionally. Let mixture cool. Then strain and pour liquid over sardines. Marinate in the refrigerator for several hours. Just before serving, garnish with grated egg yolks and pimiento strips. Serve in small bowls as a first course.

SERVES 6

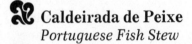 Caldeirada de Peixe
Portuguese Fish Stew

While cod is the culinary staple for the Portuguese, fish of all sorts abound. This dish calls for as many kinds of fresh fish as you can readily lay hands on—use at least three kinds, or skip the dish.

    3 pounds assorted fresh fish fillets
    1 teaspoon salt
    35-ounce can tomatoes, drained
    3 onions, chopped
    2 cloves garlic, minced
    ½ cup olive oil
    ½ teaspoon powdered ginger
    ¼ teaspoon powdered cumin
    6 tablespoons chopped fresh parsley
    2 cups water
    4 potatoes, peeled and cubed
    dash Tabasco

Sprinkle fish with salt and let stand 1 hour. Cut into chunks. Put tomatoes, onions, garlic, oil, ginger, and cumin in a soup pot. Simmer for 20 minutes. Add half the chopped parsley and the water and bring to a boil. Add the potatoes; cook for 10 minutes. Add the fish chunks, reduce heat, and simmer until fish is tender, about 15 minutes. Add the Tabasco and gently stir to mix. Just before serving, sprinkle with the rest of the parsley.

SERVES 6

Poultry

Arroz con Pollo, Surinam-Style

In Surinam, along the northern coast of South America, arroz con pollo takes on a very unusual character. Chili powder is one of the surprising additions. Small bowls of chutney and chopped, seeded cucumber are excellent accompaniments to this dish.

    2-pound chicken, cut into 8 pieces
    2 leeks, sliced
    1 bay leaf
    2 sprigs fresh parsley
    2 teaspoons salt
    10 black peppercorns, crushed
    4 tablespoons peanut oil
    2 onions, finely chopped
    2 cloves garlic, minced
    1½ cups rice
    1½ cups chopped cooked shrimp (½ pound)
    1 cup crabmeat (½ pound)
    1 cup chopped cooked ham
    2 teaspoons powdered coriander
    1 teaspoon powdered cumin
    1 teaspoon chili powder
    ¼ teaspoon freshly grated nutmeg
    ½ cup chopped unsalted peanuts

Put chicken, leeks, bay leaf, parsley, salt, and peppercorns in a large pot of water (at least 7 cups). Bring to a boil, cover, and simmer 1 hour, or until chicken is tender. Remove chicken and let cool. Pour off 4 cups of the stock, reserving the rest for another use. Remove chicken skin, and slice meat into thin strips; discard bones.

In a heavy casserole, heat the oil and sauté onions and garlic until golden. Add the rice and brown lightly, stirring frequently. Add the 4 cups of stock, chicken, shrimp, crabmeat, ham, coriander, cumin, chili powder, and nutmeg. Mix well, cover, and simmer over low heat about 15 minutes, or until most of the liquid has been absorbed. Just before serving, stir in the peanuts.

SERVES 6 TO 8

ℬ Caribbean Arroz con Pollo

Here is an island version of arroz con pollo. Asterisked items can be replaced by 3 tablespoons of *sofrito*, a Latin seasoning mixture available in specialty food shops.

> 1 teaspoon oregano
> 2 black peppercorns, cracked
> 1 clove garlic, mashed
> 3 teaspoons salt
> 2 teaspoons olive oil
> 1 teaspoon vinegar
> 2½-pound frying chicken, cut into 8 pieces
> 2 tablespoons lard or olive oil
> ¼ cup chopped ham
> 1-inch cube salt pork or 1 slice bacon, chopped
> *1 onion, chopped
> *1 bell pepper, seeded and chopped
> *1 fresh green chili, seeded and chopped
> *2 sprigs cilantro (fresh coriander) or flat-leaf parsley,
>   chopped

¼ teaspoon annatto seed or other saffron-color agent
4 tomatoes, chopped
2 cups long-grain rice
3 cups chicken stock, or 2 cups water and 1 cup white
    wine
10-ounce package frozen peas
4-ounce jar whole pimientos

Combine the oregano, peppercorns, garlic, salt, 2 teaspoons olive oil, and vinegar; rub the chicken pieces with the mixture. Set aside in a bowl.

In a deep kettle heat the 2 tablespoons of lard or olive oil. Add chicken and brown lightly on all sides. Add the ham and salt pork or bacon and brown over high heat.

Add the onion, bell pepper, chili, and cilantro or parsley (or the *sofrito*), and lower heat to medium. Add the annatto, tomatoes, and rice, and stir for 5 minutes. Add the stock or water and wine; when mixture begins to boil, lower heat and simmer, covered, for 15 minutes. With a wooden fork, *not* a spoon, lift from bottom to stir and fluff rice.

Add peas in a decorative crisscross pattern, cover, and simmer over very low heat for 5 minutes or more. Drain pimientos, and cut into strips ¼ inch wide. Just before serving, add the bright red pimientos in spaces around the peas. Serve piping hot.

SERVES 4

Oryekhovyi Sous
Russian Chicken with Walnut Sauce

A different way to treat a chicken, this dish from Soviet Georgia is succulent, crunchy, and delicious. Serve with kasha or rice.

    3 tablespoons vegetable oil
    1 clove garlic
    ½ cup plus 1 tablespoon flour
    salt and freshly ground black pepper
    2-pound chicken, cut into 8 pieces
    2 tablespoons butter
    1 clove garlic, minced
    1 onion, chopped
    ½ cup chopped walnuts
    1 cup chicken stock
    1 tablespoon white vinegar
    ⅛ teaspoon powdered allspice
    ⅛ teaspoon powdered cinnamon
    ⅛ teaspoon freshly grated nutmeg
    4 sprigs fresh parsley, minced

In a large pot, heat oil over medium-high flame. Brown garlic clove and discard. Season ½ cup flour with ½ teaspoon salt and a generous grinding of black pepper and dredge chicken pieces in the flour. Brown the chicken pieces. Cover and cook over medium heat until tender (about 25 minutes). Remove and keep warm on a platter.

Add butter to pot and add garlic, onion, and walnuts. Stir until onions are golden. Sprinkle with 1 tablespoon flour and cook 3 minutes longer, stirring occasionally. Add chicken stock, vinegar, and spices. Cook until sauce is smooth and slightly thickened. Add salt and pepper to taste. Pour sauce over chicken, and sprinkle liberally with minced parsley.

SERVES 4

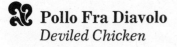

Pollo en Jugo de Naranja y Piña
Chicken in Orange Juice with Pineapple

From tropical Mexico comes this quite unusual dish with a mild sweet-hot tang. It is fine made in advance, and reheats admirably.

½ cup raisins
1 cup orange juice
salt and generous grinding black pepper
½ cup flour
2-pound chicken, cut into 8 pieces
3 tablespoons lard or vegetable oil
½ cup almonds, blanched
½ cup drained and chopped canned pineapple
2 tablespoons sugar
¼ teaspoon powdered cinnamon
¼ teaspoon powdered cloves
½ teaspoon salt

Soak the raisins in the orange juice for 1 hour. Mix salt and pepper into flour. Dredge chicken pieces in the seasoned flour. Heat the lard or oil in a heavy skillet and sauté chicken until golden brown on all sides. Transfer chicken to a shallow baking dish. Add all remaining ingredients to the raisins and orange juice and dribble the mixture over the chicken. Bake in a 325° F. oven for 30 minutes, basting frequently. Raise heat to 400° F. and cook for 10 minutes longer.

SERVES 4

Pollo Fra Diavolo
Deviled Chicken

This deviled chicken from Sicily is a variation of chicken cacciatore, with that dash of red so dear to Sicilians. The green pasta is also a novel touch.

2 tablespoons olive oil
3½- to 4-pound chicken, cut into 8 pieces
1 large onion, chopped
4 cloves garlic, mashed
35-ounce can plum tomatoes
8-ounce can tomato sauce
½ cup dry white wine
½ cup chopped fresh flat-leaf parsley
2 teaspoons salt
¼ teaspoon dried red pepper flakes
generous grinding black pepper
1 pound spinach noodles

In a large skillet, heat oil and brown the chicken pieces. Remove chicken, pour off all but 3 tablespoons fat, and sauté the onion and garlic for about 3 minutes, until onion turns golden. Add all other ingredients except the noodles. Replace chicken in skillet. Cover tightly and simmer 1 to 1½ hours, until chicken is tender. Stir occasionally and add more liquid (half water, half wine) if mixture is dry. When chicken is almost done, cook the pasta *al dente* according to package directions. Drain and put on heated platter. Add the bird to the nest, and cover with sauce.

SERVES 4 TO 6

🍲 Rum Crumb Chicken

This sumptuous dish is a North American version of a Caribbean specialty. I like it best served over dry steamed rice.

4 whole chicken breasts, skinned, boned, split, and flattened
8 tablespoons Major Grey–type chutney
1 cup fine bread crumbs
1 scant teaspoon dried red pepper flakes
½ teaspoon salt
generous grinding black pepper
½ cup dark rum
¼ pound (1 stick) butter

Heat oven to 350° F. Lay chicken breasts flat on work surface. Spoon 1 tablespoon of chutney onto each breast, fold over, and fasten each breast with a wooden toothpick. Mix crumbs with the red pepper flakes, salt, and black pepper in a bowl. Dip each piece of folded chicken into the rum and then roll in seasoned crumbs. In a large, heavy skillet, melt butter and add chicken. Brown on both sides. Put the chicken into a baking dish, and pour over it any remaining rum and crumbs. Cover tightly with foil and bake for 20 minutes.

SERVES 4

Thai Heavenly Chicken

Some of the hottest food on earth is served in Thailand. Nonetheless, it is a superior cuisine. Not every dish is too blistery for an American palate. This delightful main course is no more than rosily piquant. Serve it with stir-fried green vegetables, slivered green beans, or braised celery.

2 whole chicken breasts, skinned, halved, and boned
4 whole scallions, minced
¼ cup water
1 teaspoon salt
1½ teaspoons powdered ginger
2 tablespoons cornstarch
2 cups chicken broth
3 tablespoons soy sauce
¼ teaspoon dried red pepper flakes
2 teaspoons minced fresh ginger

Place chicken breasts between two sheets of waxed paper, and pound with a mallet or knife handle until thin. Set aside. In a bowl, make a paste of the minced scallions, water, salt, and powdered ginger. Spread paste on chicken breasts and wrap each one separately in foil. Steam for 30 minutes.

Meanwhile, mix the cornstarch with a tablespoon or two of the broth in a saucepan and stir until smooth. Add the rest of the broth and cook over low heat, stirring until thick. Add the soy sauce, pepper flakes, and fresh ginger, and simmer for 5 minutes. When chicken is done, put on serving platter, slit foil packs, and pour sauce over chicken.

SERVES 2

ℵ Spicy Indian Chicken

In India, it is the Madras curries that are tomato-based. This adaptation, more at home in the United States, is also delicious. The rich tomato sauce can be used in many other dishes as well.

To make the tomato sauce:
2 tablespoons butter
3 onions, finely chopped
4 tomatoes, peeled, seeded, and chopped
generous grinding black pepper
pinch sugar
4 sprigs fresh parsley
pinch thyme
1 bay leaf

To prepare the chicken:
2 onions, chopped
4 cloves garlic, chopped
3 quarter-size pieces fresh ginger, chopped
2 inches stick cinnamon, broken into bits
½ teaspoon powdered coriander
6 whole cloves
2 bay leaves, crumbled
½ teaspoon dried red pepper flakes
¼ cup water, chicken broth, or white wine
½ pound (2 sticks) unsalted butter
1 plump fryer, cut into 8 pieces

Make the tomato sauce first: In a heavy skillet, melt butter over medium heat, and sauté the onions until golden. Add the tomatoes and all other sauce ingredients. Simmer over low heat, covered, for 10 minutes, stirring occasionally. Uncover and increase heat to medium; cook mixture for 10 minutes more, or until liquid has evaporated, and mixture has reduced and thickened. You should have about 2 cups.

Crush in a mortar, or purée quickly in a blender, the onions, garlic, ginger, cinnamon, coriander, cloves, bay leaves, and pepper flakes. Add the water, broth, or wine and blend to form a paste. Reserve.

In a large, heavy pot, melt the butter over a medium-high flame, and brown the chicken pieces on all sides. Remove chicken to a plate. Lower heat to medium, add the paste to the pan, and sauté for 5 minutes. Add the tomato sauce and bring to a boil, scraping in brown bits from sides of pan. Lower heat to simmer, cover, and cook for 20 minutes, stirring occasionally. Return the chicken to the pot, and stir to coat chicken with sauce. Cover, and simmer for 30 minutes, or until meat is tender, turning chicken pieces occasionally.

SERVES 4

🎜 Tipsy Chicken

This is not the same as the Chinese "drunken chicken." You might describe it as "baked martini chicken," since it demands the juniper-flavor elixir known as gin in the marinade. Since the chicken marinates for a day or more, you might want to buy the mushrooms fresh at the time of cooking. This dish goes well with steamed rice or a pilaf.

        salt
        2½-pound chicken, quartered
        generous dash cayenne
        1 onion, thinly sliced
        2 carrots, thinly sliced
        4 shallots, minced
        2 cups gin
        ½ pound fresh mushrooms, sliced
        butter

Lightly salt the chicken, add cayenne, and place in a casserole. Cover it with a layer of sliced onions, a layer of sliced carrots, and a layer of minced shallots. Carefully pour the gin over all. Marinate for a day or two in the refrigerator, turning the chicken occasionally. Preheat oven to 350° F. Before putting bird with the marinade in the oven, cover with the mushrooms and dot with butter. Roast uncovered approximately 45 minutes until browned.

SERVES 3 OR 4

🎜 Curried Chicken Salad

A refreshing luncheon for a summer day. Serve with hot crusty bread and wine.

> 2 large whole chicken breasts, halved
> 2 stalks celery, sliced
> 2 carrots, sliced
> 1 large onion, sliced
> 6 black peppercorns, cracked
> ½ teaspoon salt
> 4 whole lettuce leaves
> 1 small bell pepper, finely chopped
> 2 apples, peeled, cored, and diced
> 2 stalks celery, minced
> 3 whole scallions, finely chopped
> ¾ cup mayonnaise
> 1 rounded tablespoon curry powder (p. 13)
> 1 teaspoon lemon juice
> dash Tabasco
> salt and freshly ground black pepper to taste

Place chicken breasts, sliced celery, carrots, onion, peppercorns, and salt in a large saucepan. Cover with water and bring to a boil. Lower heat and simmer for 20 minutes. Remove chicken from water, and reserve stock for other uses. Cool chicken until you can handle it comfortably. Remove skin; bone chicken and cut into bite-size pieces. Put the chicken pieces in a large salad bowl on top of lettuce leaves. Add the bell pepper, apples, minced celery, and scallions as garnish.

In a small bowl, combine mayonnaise, curry powder, lemon juice, Tabasco, and salt and pepper. Blend thoroughly. Pour over chicken and mix well. Chill for at least 1 hour before serving.

SERVES 4

 Doro Wat
Ethiopian Chicken

My friend Tekle Mariam Woldemikael (Tekle, son of Michael) tells me this is the national chicken dish in his land. It is equally authentic as a sauté dish or a stew. I have made my own adaptation, which I think works well. Doro Wat should be served with *Enjera*, lacy buckwheat pancakes (following recipe).

    2 tablespoons butter
    4 onions, chopped
    2 frying chickens, quartered
    4 cloves garlic, chopped
    4 fresh hot green peppers, seeded and chopped, or 1 rounded
        teaspoon dried red pepper flakes
    1 inch fresh ginger, peeled and minced
    3 ripe tomatoes, chopped
    8 hard-boiled eggs

In a large skillet (or two smaller ones), melt the butter and fry the onions until they become translucent, about 8 minutes. Remove from skillet, and in same pan sear chicken over high heat, turning until all sides are browned.

Now top the chicken with the onions, and add remaining ingredients except for the eggs. Add 1 cup water, turn heat to low, and simmer for at least 1 hour. Add a splash more water if necessary to keep chicken moist. When the dish is ready, an oily film will form over the top.

Meanwhile hard-boil the eggs, about 20 minutes, cool in cold water, and peel. Make eight vertical slits through the white of each egg (not the yolk) and add eggs to the chicken pan,

Serve while hot—one piece of chicken and 1 egg per person, preferably served over an *enjera*.

SERVES 8

๕๒ Enjera
Ethiopian Lace Pancakes

Enjera are thin buckwheat pancakes, which are used as tortillas are—torn in bits to scoop up food in lieu of knife and fork; they are even sometimes used as plates.

In Ethiopia, when Doro Wat is served, it is either presented on one huge *enjera* or several smaller individual ones. The idea is to give each guest a piece of chicken, an egg, and some of the onion-tomato mixture on top of the *enjera*. A second *enjera* is used to sop up juices or may be buttered and eaten as bread.

While Tekle's grandmother makes a dough starter that sours a few days before she uses it for the pancakes, the club soda is a modern time-saver that achieves a similar lacy effect. *Enjera*, to be real, must have "eyes" in them. The thinner and lacier, the more authentic.

¾ cup buckwheat flour (whole-wheat flour is a barely
   acceptable substitute)
¾ cup all-purpose flour
3 teaspoons baking powder
½ teaspoon salt
1 egg, lightly beaten
2 tablespoons melted butter
1 cup club soda

Mix the flours with baking powder and salt. Stir in beaten egg. Add the club soda all at once, stirring quickly to get a thin batter. If necessary, add more club soda until batter is the consistency of thin cream. Make pancakes at once, while soda still froths.

Test heated griddle or iron skillet by tossing on a few drops of water. If they dance about as bubbles, the surface is ready.

Spoon onto buttered griddle about 2 tablespoons of batter per pancake. Cover immediately and cook for 1 or 2 minutes, until bottom is golden and top is filled with "eyes." Do not cook top side. Put each pancake on a serving plate kept in a warm oven. Make 16 pancakes.

When you are ready to serve the Doro Wat, give each guest an *enjera*; put a piece of chicken, an egg, and some onion-tomato mixture on top; place another *enjera* on the side of the plate.

SERVES 8

🎵 Green Pepper Duck, Four Seasons

Unripened (green) peppercorns go uniquely well with duck. We were pleased to get this distinguished recipe from The Four Seasons restaurant in New York. When you buy green peppercorns, buy them in cans, not in jars. Sunlight destroys their flavor.

2 onions, cut into large cubes
½ stalk celery, cut into 1-inch pieces
2 cloves garlic, mashed
½ teaspoon minced fresh basil
½ teaspoon marjoram
½ teaspoon thyme
2 ducklings, 4 to 4½ pounds each, cleaned
1 rounded teaspoon salt
1 quart water or chicken stock
½ cup port
½ cup Burgundy
1 cup sour cream
2 tablespoons green Madagascar peppercorns
¼ pound (1 stick) unsalted butter, softened

Heat oven to 325° F. Cover the bottom of a large roasting pan with the onions, celery, garlic, basil, marjoram, and thyme. Salt ducklings lightly and place them in the pan on their backs. Add water or chicken stock so that the leg joints are barely covered (about 1 inch). Cook for 1 to 1½ hours, checking that the birds don't take on any color. If necessary, cover with foil. Remove ducks and cook until lukewarm, reserving stock for later. Remove all skin carefully in as large pieces as possible.

Bone ducks, keeping wings attached to breasts and legs attached to thighs. Place boned ducks on a snug covered casserole. Place in 200° F. oven to keep warm.

Carefully remove all excess fat from the skin; then cut skin into ⅓-inch-thick strips and place under broiler until crunchy-crisp. Reserve for garnish. Skim fat from the cooking liquid.

Put remaining bones, trimmings, and cooking liquid in a large pot; add port and Burgundy. Boil over high heat to reduce sauce to 2 cups. Strain through a fine sieve. Place liquid aside, cover, and keep warm.

In a shallow pan or casserole, gently melt the sour cream, stirring constantly with a wire whisk. (Don't boil or it will curdle.) When sour cream is warm and smooth, turn off heat and slowly stir in the 2 cups of sauce base and all but 1 teaspoon of the green peppercorns. With a wooden spoon mash the peppercorns as you push the sauce through a fine strainer. Be sure to get all the peppercorns through strainer and into sauce. Warm sauce over low heat. Whip in the butter, a little at a time.

Pour heated sauce over ducks and sprinkle on the remaining green peppercorns. Place the crisp skin on top. Serve very hot.

SERVES 4

Beef

Roast Beef, Trinidad-Style

For this dish, which is a surprising way to treat beef, use the best cut you can afford. Serve with rice or mashed potatoes.

    4 pounds beef for roasting
    4 cloves garlic, mashed
    1 tablespoon powdered coriander
    1 teaspoon cayenne
    1 teaspoon cumin seed
    1 teaspoon powdered ginger
    ½ teaspoon powdered cinnamon
    2 bay leaves, crushed
    2 tablespoons white vinegar
    2 tablespoons fresh lemon juice
    salt to taste
    1 cup boiling water
    2 tablespoons vegetable oil
    2 onions, thinly sliced

Prick meat with a fork. Combine all ingredients except the water, oil, and onions, and blend to a paste. A few seconds in a blender will do it; otherwise use a mortar and pestle. Rub the meat well with the paste and let meat rest for 4 hours or more.

Preheat oven to 325° F. Put meat in a roasting pan, and pour 1 cup boiling water around it. Cover and roast for 2 hours.

About 10 minutes before meat is done, heat oil in a large skillet. Add onions and fry until crisp. Remove beef from roasting pan, slice it, and add to pan with the onions. Stir well, add drippings from roasting pan, and stir again. Simmer for 5 minutes, and serve.

SERVES 6

Bavarian Pot Roast

This is so good even a Bavarian would not consider the beer used in the sauce as wasted. Spice this dish with a generous hand, and serve it with noodles.

3 strips bacon, fried
4 pounds boneless chuck or round steak
1 tablespoon sugar
1 tablespoon white vinegar
1 rounded teaspoon powdered cinnamon
1 rounded teaspoon powdered ginger
12 ounces beer
12-ounce can tomato sauce or ¾ cup Fresh Tomato Sauce
    (p. 227)
1 large onion, chopped
1 bay leaf
1 rounded teaspoon salt
generous grinding black pepper
4 gingersnaps, crushed, or 2 tablespoons flour

Fry bacon in a large pot over high heat. Add the meat and brown. In a large bowl, mix all other ingredients, except gingersnaps or flour, and pour over the meat. Lower heat, and simmer, covered, until meat is tender (about 2 hours).

To thicken the gravy, remove meat to a platter and stir in either the crushed gingersnaps or the flour. Pour gravy over pot roast, and serve immediately.

SERVES 8 TO 10

✥ Cardamom Roast

Cardamom is an expensive but individualistic spice that is well worth experimenting with. Its strong, pungent flavor is essential to good curry powder. Here it is used in a most unusual recipe offered by Harriet Lembeck, a petite bundle of energy who is active in the Wine and Food Society and teaches the famous Beverage Program course "Spirits of the World."

¼ cup lard or other shortening
5 pounds lean beef pot roast
2⅓ cups water
1 cup red wine vinegar
1 cup dry white wine
½ cup brown sugar, packed
3 onions, chopped
2 tablespoons pickling spice
2 teaspoons powdered cardamom
⅓ cup flour

Heat lard or shortening in deep skillet and brown meat on all sides. Skim off excess fat. Add 2 cups water, vinegar, wine, brown sugar, onions, pickling spice, and cardamom. Cover and simmer for 3 to 4 hours, until tender. Remove meat and keep warm. Strain stock into a saucepan, and place over a medium flame. Blend flour and ⅓ cup water and stir into stock. Continue to stir until sauce thickens. Pour sauce over meat and serve immediately.

SERVES 8

✥ Sauerbraten
German Sour Pot Roast

Sauerbraten is a misnomer, since the dish is not at all sour, although the gravy is delightfully tart. In olden times, tough meat had to marinate for days. The dish still benefits from marinating longer than the bare minimum of 24 hours.

4-pound boneless beef roast (rump, chuck, or bottom
    round), trimmed of fat
1 cup dry red wine
1 cup red wine vinegar
2 cups cold water
1 large onion, thinly sliced
8 black peppercorns, cracked
1 bay leaf
4 whole cloves
4 sprigs fresh parsley
½ teaspoon salt
2 tablespoons flour
generous grinding black pepper
3 tablespoons lard or oil
1 onion, minced
1 carrot, diced
8 gingersnaps, crumbled

Put the beef in a large bowl. In a large pot, combine the wine,
vinegar, water, onion, peppercorns, bay leaf, cloves, parsley, and
salt. Bring to a boil, and pour over the beef. Allow to cool and
marinate in the refrigerator for 1 to 4 days. Turn the meat
twice a day.

When ready to cook, take the meat from the marinade and
pat dry. Strain marinade and reserve. Rub meat with flour and
season with generous grinding black pepper. Melt lard or oil in
a Dutch oven or iron kettle, and brown meat on all sides over
medium-high flame. Remove meat. Add minced onion and carrot
to the pot and sauté for 5 minutes. Add 3 cups of the marinade
and bring to a boil. Return the meat to the kettle. Cover and
simmer until meat is tender, about 2 hours. Remove meat and
place on a warm platter. Bring the liquid to a boil and stir in the
gingersnap crumbs. Cook for 1 minute more until sauce thickens,
and pour into a gravy boat. Slice the meat and serve immediately,
accompanied by the sauce.

SERVES 6 TO 8

🎵 Caribbean Corned Beef and Cabbage

Not really so very different from our familiar corned beef dish, but the spices give a flair to this sometimes bland entrée. Serve with rice or potatoes.

    2 pounds corned brisket of beef
    1 large onion, quartered
    4 whole cloves
    4 medium potatoes, cubed (optional)
    salt
    2 pounds green cabbage, shredded
    1 cup finely chopped onions
    1 cup chopped whole scallions
    2 cloves garlic, minced
    2 dried red peppers, seeded and chopped
    ¼ cup olive oil
    freshly ground black pepper

Soak the beef in cold water to cover for 30 minutes. Drain and rinse. Cut into 1-inch cubes and place in a large pot with water to cover. Stud each onion quarter with a clove, and add to pot. Cover and simmer until meat is tender, about 2 hours. During last 30 minutes, cubed potatoes may be added.

Bring a large pot of water to a boil, add 1 teaspoon salt, and cook the cabbage about 5 minutes. Set meat on a platter and keep warm.

Drain off meat stock, but reserve 1 cup of it. In a small skillet, mix 1 cup stock with onions, scallions, garlic, red peppers, and olive oil. Add salt and pepper to taste. Blend well, heat through, and pour over cabbage on serving platter. Arrange beef cubes over cabbage, and serve at once.

SERVES 6

♋ Steak Bernal

A very dear friend permitted me to include this tangy dish in my book as long as I named it after him. I so do. This dish must be cooked as swiftly as possible if it is to be perfect.

> 12-ounce sirloin steak
> 1 teaspoon finest olive oil
> 3 tablespoons butter
> 1 teaspoon dry mustard
> 1 teaspoon chopped chives
> ½ teaspoon salt
> freshly ground black pepper
> juice of ½ lemon
> 1 teaspoon Worcestershire sauce
> 2-ounce jigger Cognac
> 1 teaspoon chopped fresh parsley

Trim all fat from the meat, and pound it until it's large and very thin. In a large skillet, heat the oil and 2 tablespoons of the butter. Mix in the mustard and chives. Add the steak to the sizzling mixture, quickly scorch it, then salt and lavishly pepper it. Cook no more than 1½ minutes per side to keep steak rare. Remove steak to a hot platter and keep warm. To the skillet add the lemon juice, Worcestershire sauce, and remaining 1 tablespoon butter. As soon as the butter melts, gently warm the Cognac in a large serving spoon, ignite, and dribble over the pan. Quickly sprinkle in the parsley, blend rapidly, pour over steak, and serve.

SERVES 1 TO 2

♋ Steak au Poivre

As with garlic in some dishes, this one requires more pepper than you would think possible—yet the result is pungent rather than blistery. Note that its purity remains unsullied by the addition of any cream.

2 tablespoons coarsely ground black pepper
1 club steak, trimmed of all fat
salt
1 teaspoon butter
1 teaspoon Worcestershire sauce
1 teaspoon lemon juice
dash Tabasco
1 tablespoon Cognac
pinch chopped fresh parsley and chives

Sprinkle pepper lavishly on each side of the steak and press it into the meat, using the heel of your hand. Let stand for 30 minutes.

Sprinkle salt on bottom of a large iron skillet, and turn heat high until salt begins to turn brown. Add the steak and cook 30 seconds on each side, then turn off heat, leaving the pan on the stove. Dot the steak with butter and add the Worcestershire, lemon juice, and Tabasco. Warm the Cognac in a spoon or small dish, light it, and pour over meat. Sprinkle steak with parsley and chives and serve smoking hot.

SERVES 1

❧ Mexican-Style Steak

A simple, familiar dish from South of the Border. Knowledgeable guests will anticipate rice and beans as an accompaniment.

¼ teaspoon salt
1 teaspoon chili powder
½ cup flour, plus 1 scant tablespoon
1 pound round steak, ½ inch thick
1 tablespoon olive or vegetable oil
1 onion, chopped
1 clove garlic, mashed
1 cup coarsely chopped fresh tomatoes
1 tablespoon white wine, stock, or water

Mix salt, chili powder, and ½ cup flour into a smooth blend, and beat into steak with the butt end of a knife. In a large skillet, heat the oil and sauté the onion and garlic for 3 minutes. Add steak and quickly brown both sides over high heat. Add tomatoes and water to cover. Cover skillet and simmer 30 minutes, or until meat is tender. Remove meat to a hot platter. Make gravy by blending 1 scant tablespoon flour with 1 tablespoon white wine, stock, or water. Stir to mix well, add to skillet, blend, and bring to a boil. Pour into a gravy boat, and serve immediately with meat.

SERVES 2

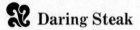 **Daring Steak**

One more purely American adaptation of an East Indian dish. In a land where cows are sacred to many, I doubt if you'd find a recipe for curried steaks, which this approximates.

>   1 orange
>   2 cloves garlic
>   ½ cup dry red wine
>   2 tablespoons vegetable oil
>   2 tablespoons soy sauce
>   1 tablespoon vinegar
>   1½ teaspoons salt
>   ½ teaspoon turmeric
>   ½ teaspoon cayenne
>   ½ teaspoon powdered ginger
>   ½ teaspoon dry mustard
>   steaks for 4 persons

With a sharp paring knife, cut 2 strips of peel 2 inches long by ½ inch wide off the orange. Chop strips into very fine bits. Mince garlic cloves into the orange peel, and stir to let peel absorb garlic juices. In a large, shallow bowl, mix peel, garlic, and all other ingredients (except steaks) to make a marinade.

Place steaks in bowl, cover with marinade, and let stand for at least 1 hour, turning once. Broil steaks, brushing them frequently with the marinade until steaks are as rare as you like them.

SERVES 4

𝕾 Tournedos Caprice

Among America's great restaurants is Le Cirque, situated in the Mayfair House Hotel in New York City. One of the things that keeps Le Cirque great is its continuing endeavor to enliven a fastidious menu with innovations. Few of its continental specialties are spicy, but this one is; it is a lovely extravaganza on the Steak au Poivre theme.

Prepare in advance
4 mushroom caps, preferably carved decoratively
4 crêpes (following recipe)
4 French-Fried Onion Rings (p. 194)
2 large white turnips, peeled
1 pound fresh spinach, cooked and chopped

4 tournedos of beef, 8 ounces each
2 tablespoons cracked black peppercorns
¼ teaspoon salt
5 tablespoons butter
½ cup veal or chicken stock
4 tablespoons brandy
4 tablespoons heavy cream
4 cherry tomatoes

Carve mushroom caps and set aside. Keep prepared crêpes warm while you prepare the rest of the ingredients. Make onion rings just before assembling the dish and keep warm. Steam turnips for 5 minutes and lightly sauté them. Cut them in half and scoop out centers to form four baskets. Cook spinach 2 minutes, fill turnip baskets, and keep warm.

Lay the tournedos flat and mash the cracked peppercorns into them. Sprinkle with salt. Heat 1 tablespoon of the butter in a skillet over high flame. Sauté the tournedos, removing them while they are still extremely rare. Keep warm on a hot plate.

Add the stock, the remaining 4 tablespoons butter, brandy, and cream; deglaze the skillet.

On a large heated serving platter, dress the tournedos with the deglazed sauce. Cover each tournedo with a crêpe, 1 onion ring, and 1 mushroom cap. Serve each tournedo on a heated plate. On the side, garnish with 1 cherry tomato and 1 turnip basket stuffed with spinach.

Serve very hot.

SERVES 4

🎜 Crêpes

There are many kinds of crêpes; the following is one of the simpler all-purpose recipes. It is important to let the batter stand for an hour or two before using it so that every tiny bubble will evaporate. This batter will improve with age, and it will keep, if covered and refrigerated, up to a week.

3 eggs
¾ cup all-purpose flour
pinch salt
1 teaspoon sugar and 1 teaspoon grated orange rind
   (optional, for dessert crêpes only)
1 cup milk
2 tablespoons melted butter
butter for the skillet

Beat eggs lightly and add alternately, beating constantly, the dry ingredients and the milk. Or put all ingredients, with exception of melted butter, into a blender and blend well. (Add sugar and orange rind if making dessert crêpes.) Stir in the melted butter. Let the batter sit for an hour or two, or more.

Heat a heavy skillet over medium-high heat (8-inch for

filled crêpes, 6-inch for dessert crêpes). Add dot of butter and tilt pan to cover bottom with layer of fat. Spoon in the least amount of batter possible (about 2 tablespoons) and tilt pan immediately to let batter flow thinly to all edges—the thinner the batter, the better the crêpe. Use the same amount of batter for each crêpe.

In less than 1 minute the top of the crêpe should become dry. Either slip a thin spatula beneath crêpe and flip it over for a few seconds, or remove it to a plate. Crêpes stack well if they are cooked on both sides. You can cook them in advance and keep them wrapped in waxed paper until ready to use.

MAKES ABOUT 20 TO 24 CRÊPES

🙂 Steak Strips Saté

This is a slightly Americanized version of a Japanese favorite: delicious nonetheless. This can be served with Indonesian Saté (p. 129), or separately, as a main dish.

    2 pounds beef sirloin, cut into 1-inch lengths
    ½ cup soy sauce
    ¼ cup sesame oil
    1 small onion, minced
    1 clove garlic, minced
    4 tablespoons sesame seed

Slice the meat and set aside. Mix together in a large bowl the soy sauce, sesame oil, onion, and garlic. Marinate the meat in this mixture for at least 2 hours, tossing meat occasionally. Meanwhile, crush the sesame seed and toast in a small skillet over a medium-high flame for 2 or 3 minutes, until lightly browned.

When ready to cook, remove meat strips from marinade and roll them in the sesame seed. Broil over charcoal or sauté in a skillet over a high flame for 1 or 2 minutes.

SERVES 4 TO 6

ℜ Prosperity Beef

This is an example of Francis Cheong's unique adaptations of
the classic Chinese cuisine, a dish designed to ornament his
special New Year's menu served at his two Long Island restaurants, Chi Ling and Cheong's Garden. The cabbage leaf is dis-
pensable for the cooking, but indispensable for the color of the
dish. Dried tangerine peel and rice vinegar are available at
Chinese markets or see Mail-Order Sources.

¼ pound flank steak
5 dried black mushrooms

Marinade
1 beaten egg
1 teaspoon dry sherry
2 teaspoons cornstarch

Vegetables
3 quarter-size slices fresh ginger
1 tablespoon minced dried tangerine peel or orange peel
1 small bell pepper, cut into triangles
2 whole scallions, cut into ½-inch pieces
1 clove garlic, mashed
1 large cabbage leaf, cut into triangles

Sauce
4 teaspoons soy sauce
1½ teaspoons sugar
1½ teaspoons rice vinegar or white wine vinegar
2 teaspoons dry sherry
2 small dried red peppers, seeded and minced
2½ teaspoons cornstarch
dash sesame oil
freshly ground black pepper
¼ cup water from soaking mushrooms

½ cup peanut oil

Cut the steak into strips 1½ inches long and ¼ inch wide.

Soak the dried mushrooms for 30 minutes in a small amount of warm water. Drain, rinse, destem, and thin-slice them, reserving the liquid for use in the sauce. Mix marinade ingredients, and marinate meat strips for 30 minutes. Prepare all the vegetables. Mix sauce ingredients and set aside in separate bowl.

Heat the peanut oil in wok or deep cast-iron skillet to just short of smoking. Drain meat and add it to oil. Stir-fry for 2 minutes, flipping beef strips vigorously. Remove beef, drain the oil, and put vegetables in wok. Stir-fry for 2 minutes over high heat. Put the beef back in the pan, pour sauce over all, and stir-fry for about 1 minute or until sauce begins to thicken.

SERVES 2

🦋 Rostelyos
Hungarian Braised Beef

A Hungarian national dish, and justifiably so.

Four 6-ounce slices top round
2 tablespoons flour
¼ pound lard (or 4 tablespoons each butter and vegetable oil)
1 large onion, coarsely chopped
1 clove garlic, mashed
½ teaspoon caraway seed
1 tablespoon Hungarian paprika
½ cup dry white wine
½ cup white vinegar
2 tomatoes, diced
2 bell peppers, diced
2 medium potatoes, diced
salt and freshly ground black pepper
½ pound lean bacon, sliced

Pound beef slices until fairly thin. Dredge in flour. Heat lard (or butter and oil) and sear the meat over high heat. Remove meat and set aside. Pour off all but 1 tablespoon of fat. In the same pan, turn heat to low and wilt the onion. Add garlic, caraway seed, and paprika. Add wine, vinegar, tomatoes, peppers, and potatoes, and simmer for 10 minutes. Add salt and pepper to taste. Meanwhile, line the bottom of a heavy iron pot with the bacon strips. Place meat on top; add vegetable mixture. Cover, and cook over low heat until meat is done, about 1 hour. If vegetables are not entirely covered by liquid, or if liquid evaporates during cooking, add water to cover.

SERVES 4

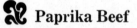 Paprika Beef

An easy dish to make in quantity, merely by literally beefing up the ingredients. It is filling and has a pleasant tang. The Hungarian paprika is crucial. Serve over rice or noodles, adding a dollop of sour cream to each portion as served.

    2 tablespoons lard or bacon drippings
    6 onions, coarsely chopped
    2 cloves garlic, chopped
    2 pounds stewing beef, cut into 1-inch cubes
    6 carrots, cut into 2-inch rounds
    2 tablespoons Hungarian paprika
    1 teaspoon cayenne
    1 teaspoon salt
    1 cup beef stock
    1 cup sour cream

In a large pot, heat 1 tablespoon oil over medium flame, and cook onions and garlic until translucent. Remove with slotted spoon and set aside. In the same pot, brown the meat over high flame with 1 tablespoon additional oil if necessary. Return onions and garlic to pot, and add all other ingredients except sour cream. Bring to a boil, then reduce flame to very low, cover pot, and simmer for 2 hours, or until meat is very tender.

SERVES 4 TO 6

🎫 Janet's Oxtail Ragout

My wife Janet is not as interested in cooking with spices as I am. However, she does like to make this fine, unusual stew.

    2 tablespoons olive oil
    2 tablespoons butter
    joints of 1 oxtail
    8 to 10 shallots, peeled and halved
    2 red bell peppers, seeded and cut into strips
    28-ounce can whole tomatoes
    2 zucchini, scrubbed and sliced into rounds
    1 bay leaf
    ¼ teaspoon salt
    freshly ground black pepper
    1 to 3 dashes Tabasco
    1 tablespoon cornstarch dissolved in water for thickening
      (optional)

In a heavy skillet, heat the oil and butter and sear the oxtail pieces, turning them until all the pink has gone. Add the shallots and bell peppers, lower the heat, and simmer, covered, for 1 hour.

Add the tomatoes and their juice, the zucchini, bay leaf, salt, black pepper, and Tabasco. Simmer uncovered for 3 to 5 minutes, until vegetables are tender but still crunchy. Thicken the gravy with cornstarch mixture if desired.

SERVES 3 OR 4

🎫 Marie's Goulash

No Hungarian will admit that any other Hungarian can make a goulash as good as his mother's. My friend Marie Deitch has given me a version that I think is difficult to match—both for simplicity and for savor. One thing I think you should know: if the paprika is not Hungarian, the dish won't taste as good.

1 tablespoon vegetable oil
2 pounds onions, chopped (about 5 big onions)
3 pounds stewing beef, cut into 2-inch cubes
3 tablespoons Hungarian paprika
1 teaspoon freshly grated nutmeg
1 teaspoon marjoram
6-ounce can tomato paste
1 tablespoon salt
6 potatoes, peeled and cubed (optional)

In a heavy-bottomed pot, heat the oil and sauté the onions until they are translucent. Add the beef cubes and fry until they lose their redness. Add all other ingredients except potatoes. Cover tightly and simmer for 2 hours, or until beef is tender. This dish makes its own liquid as it cooks.

Cubed potatoes may be added during the last half hour; or make Hungarian-Style Little Dumplings (see recipe). Otherwise, serve with rice or noodles.

SERVES 6 TO 8

🎜 Meat Loaf

Meat loaves are like signatures: each family has its own. This one is easy to make and rewarding in its results. I forget which family signed it over to me.

Meat loaf
1 pound lean ground beef
2 onions, chopped
⅓ cup fresh bread crumbs
1 egg, beaten
1 teaspoon salt
generous grinding black pepper
2 teaspoons Worcestershire sauce
½ cup Fresh Tomato Sauce (p. 227)

Sauce
½ cup Fresh Tomato Sauce
½ cup water
2 tablespoons vinegar
2 teaspoons brown sugar
2 teaspoons dry mustard
1 teaspoon Worcestershire sauce

Heat oven to 300° F. Mix together all ingredients for meat loaf. Press firmly into baking dish. With your finger, punch holes deep into meat loaf (to store juices).

Mix together all ingredients for sauce. Pour over meat loaf. Bake for 1½ hours.

SERVES 4

Empanadas
Little Latin Meat Pies

I first encountered empanadas when, long ago, a bachelor friend of mine, half Chilean, half English, daringly served them up to fulfill a long-time boast. As I recall, he had empanadas left over, which he carefully stored in a cedar chest near his front door.

From Spain and Portugal to all along Latin America, you can delight in little meat pies—all cousins—under such names as *empadas, empadhinhas, empanadas, empanaditas,* and *empanadillas. Hinhas, ditas,* and *illas* are diminutives—little meat pies made just a bit smaller. From a hundred versions, here is one that is a notch more than merely representative.

The dough
½ pound (2 sticks) butter or margarine, chilled
6 cups flour
1 teaspoon salt
½ to ¾ cups ice water

Cut butter or margarine in four pieces and put in mixing bowl. Add flour and salt. Beat with electric beater until the mix becomes mealy. Gradually add the ice water, just enough so that the dough begins to form a ball. Chill dough at least 30 minutes before using. When ready to make crusts, divide dough in half, and knead each half about 3 minutes.

On a lightly floured surface, with a lightly floured rolling pin, roll each half of the dough in a circle about ⅛ inch thick. Cut circles about 5 inches in diameter. (Scraps can be rerolled.)

Circles can either be piled up with plastic between each layer and refrigerated or they can be filled at once. If you chill them, let them come to room temperature so they will be sticky and the folded edges will seal.

Beef filling
½ cup vegetable oil
4 onions, chopped
1½ pounds lean ground beef
2 pimientos, drained and chopped
½ cup seedless raisins
1½ teaspoons oregano
1 teaspoon Hungarian paprika
2 cloves garlic, chopped
1 teaspoon salt
freshly ground black pepper
2 hard-boiled eggs, chopped
16 or more pitted green olives (optional)

1 egg, beaten with ½ teaspoon sugar for glaze

In skillet heat oil and sauté onions until translucent. Add beef and continue sautéing until meat loses its red color, about 3 minutes. Add pimientos, raisins, oregano, paprika, garlic, salt, and a good amount of pepper; stir until well mixed. Drain off excess oil. Chill the filling in the refrigerator for 30 minutes. Add chopped hard-boiled eggs just before filling the dough. Use the olives and glaze as described below.

Preparation of empanadas: Preheat oven to 450° F. Place a mound of meat mixture on a circle of dough slightly off-center, and insert 1 olive into each mound if you like (If dough is dry, moisten edges with a bit of cold water to make a seal.)

Fold filled dough to make a turnover, and, using thumbs, seal with a crimp. Brush the top of each empanada with the egg-and-sugar glaze. Place empanadas on ungreased baking sheet with 1 inch between pies. Bake for 20 minutes until golden. Leftovers can be reheated for 10 minutes in a 350° F. oven.

MAKES ABOUT 2 DOZEN

🕸 Jamaican Meat Pies

These may be called the Caribbean version of the spicy little empanadas in the previous recipe. They are not hard to make, and they are deliciously spicy. Annatto seed may be obtained in any Spanish market or see Mail-Order Sources.

> 2 tablespoons oil
> 1 teaspoon annatto seed, or 1 heaping teaspoon
>   Hungarian paprika
> 1 pound lean ground chuck
> 1 onion, finely chopped
> 1 clove garlic, mashed
> 1 cup tomato pulp or 2 chopped tomatoes
> salt and freshly ground black pepper to taste
> 1 teaspoon dried red pepper flakes, or 1 fresh hot red
>   pepper, seeded and minced
> ½ teaspoon thyme
> 2 eggs, lightly beaten
> pie crust (p. 270, full recipe)
> 1 egg beaten with ¼ teaspoon sugar for glaze

In a large skillet, heat the oil and add the annatto seed. When seeds have given up their color, remove them with a slotted spoon, and discard. If using paprika, add it now. Then add the meat, breaking it with a fork. When meat begins to brown, add the onion and garlic; cook until onion becomes tender. Add the tomatoes, salt, black pepper, pepper flakes or hot pepper, and thyme, and stir for 5 minutes longer, or until mixture is "dry." Remove from heat, add the beaten eggs, and stir well. Cool to room temperature.

Make pastry and roll out ⅛ inch thick. Cut into 4-inch circles. Place about ¼ cup of the meat mixture on one side of each circle and fold the pastry into a half moon. Seal the edges by pinching with fingers, or use a fork to crimp. Brush with the glaze and prick tops to let steam escape. Bake on ungreased cookie sheet in a preheated 450° F. oven for 20 minutes, or until lightly browned.

For cocktails. Use 2-inch pastry circles and 1 teaspoon of meat. Bake about 15 minutes.

MAKES ABOUT TWELVE 4-INCH PATTIES

℀ Frikkadels
Malaysian–Dutch Meatballs

These are delicious served hot in a chafing dish with cocktails. They are also a luncheon dish. And they can be curried nicely, in a Coconut Sauce base (p. 222).

> 1 pound lean ground beef
> 1 thick slice bread, shredded
> 1 small onion, chopped
> 2 cloves garlic, mashed
> 2 quarter-size slices fresh ginger, minced
> ¼ teaspoon powdered cumin
> dash powdered cinnamon
> dash powdered cloves
> ½ teaspoon salt
> freshly ground black pepper
> juice of ½ lime
> 1 egg, beaten
> ½ cup bread crumbs
> 2 tablespoons butter or more, as needed

Mix the ground beef with the shredded bread, onion, garlic, ginger, cumin, cinnamon, cloves, salt, and a good amount of pepper. Moisten with the lime juice. Form into small balls, the size of marbles. Dip into the beaten egg, roll in bread crumbs, and fry in butter until browned.

SERVES 4 FOR LUNCHEON
OR 10 FOR HORS D'OEUVRES

🎵 Mom's Spanish Meat Pie

My mother was a good, plain cook who worked wonders with tough cuts of meat, which she turned into heavenly pot roasts and stews. She was not overly interested in spicy cooking, but she did have a few daring recipes. This is one of them. I always resist making it spicier than she did.

> 1 pound lean ground beef
> 1 onion, chopped
> 1 clove garlic, minced
> 1 teaspoon butter
> 8-ounce can tomato sauce
> 1 rounded teaspoon chili powder
> ½ teaspoon salt
> freshly ground black pepper to taste
> 1 large potato, cubed
> 1 rounded teaspoon cornstarch, dissolved in water
> biscuit crust (p. 253)

Fry the meat, onion, and garlic in butter until onion turns translucent. Add tomato sauce, chili powder, salt, and pepper—plus enough water to make "a nice gravy" (approximately 1 cup). Add the diced potato. Simmer over low heat about 10 minutes while you make the biscuit crust. Toward the end of the simmer add a bit of cornstarch mixture to "make a gravy as thick as you like it." (This was as exact as my mother would ever get.) If mixture is very liquid, pour off excess and serve it hot in a gravy bowl on the side.

Lay biscuit crust over the meat pie. Make slits so that the steam can escape. Bake in a 375° F. oven for about 30 minutes, or until crust is golden brown. Do not overcook.

SERVES 4

ℵ Fabulous Tamale Pie

In California boardinghouses, tamale pie is often served because it is cheap to make. On the East Coast it is considered exotic. The following recipe is composed largely of canned ingredients, and I would be ashamed to present it except that the end result, while it does not look pretty, is one of the most wonderful dishes I have ever tasted. My source for this version, which I prefer above all 1001 others, is a wonderful California cook, Virginia Molony Jackson. Accompany this pie with plenty of hot garlic bread and a fresh green salad. Masa harina is a Latin cornmeal.

> 1 teaspoon salt
> 1½ pounds lean ground beef
> 2 large onions, chopped
> 4 stalks celery, chopped
> 1 large bell pepper, seeded and chopped
> 32-ounce can tomatoes, well drained of all liquid
> 17-ounce can cream-style corn
> 2 cans tamales, coarsely broken into thirds
> 1 tablespoon chili powder
> 1 heaping tablespoon masa harina or white cornmeal
> ½ cup Monterey Jack or cheddar cheese, grated
> 4 whole scallions, chopped into ¼-inch lengths

Preheat oven to 325° F. Sprinkle salt in a large iron pot, and add chopped beef, then onions. Stir and mix over high heat, until meat loses redness and onions become translucent. Add celery and bell pepper. Add the drained tomatoes, corn, and tamales to skillet and stir gently. Add chili powder and stir again.

Take up any soupiness by sprinkling on the masa harina or cornmeal. Don't stir. Sprinkle the grated cheese over all. Bake for about 20 minutes. Just before serving, sprinkle colorful green chopped scallions over top.

SERVES 6

☙ Pakistan Kebab

Every kebab is reminiscent of its cousins, but each is delicious in its own right.

    1 pound lean ground beef
    1 tablespoon chopped fresh parsley
    1 onion, grated
    1 clove garlic, mashed
    ¼ teaspoon powdered ginger
    ¼ teaspoon turmeric
    ¼ teaspoon coriander seed
    ¼ teaspoon dried red pepper flakes
    salt to taste
    2 tablespoons yogurt, more or less

Place the beef and parsley in a bowl. Grate the onion into the bowl, using finest grater (you want the juice, not the body). Add remaining ingredients, using enough yogurt to bind the mixture. Blend thoroughly and form into sausagelike pieces. Shape and press onto skewers. Grill over charcoal or place under broiler, turning once, until meat is crusty brown on both sides and done to your taste (about 5 minutes).

SERVES 3 AS A MAIN COURSE,
6 AS AN APPETIZER

☙ Pastelillos de Carne en Parillas
Meat Patties with Bananas

We Northerners seldom combine bananas with meat. This South American recipe shows we are missing something.

    1 pound beef chuck for grinding
    ¼ pound beef suet
    1 teaspoon salt
    1 teaspoon dried red pepper flakes
    4 slices bacon
    2 ripe bananas, sliced in half lengthwise
    1 tablespoon melted butter

Grind the meat with the suet twice. Add the salt and red pepper flakes and mix well. Shape into four banana-shaped patties about 4 inches long. Circle with bacon and fasten with toothpicks. Sear meat in hot skillet. Flip meat patties and place a banana half on each patty. Brush with butter, and broil about 10 minutes, or until meat is done and bananas are golden.

SERVES 4

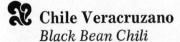 ## Chile Veracruzano
Black Bean Chili

If from an infinity of chilies there is one that can be called superlative, this is the one. Careful: it's a three-alarm chili.

    1 pound dried black beans
    1 tablespoon salt
    ¼ cup olive oil
    2 onions, chopped
    1 fresh green chili, or 1 green frying pepper, seeded and
        chopped
    3 pounds lean ground beef
    6-ounce can tomato paste
    3 tablespoons chili powder
    1 tablespoon red wine vinegar
    1 teaspoon dry mustard
    1 clove garlic, chopped
    1 teaspoon celery seed
    ½ teaspoon cumin seed
    dash cayenne
    generous grinding black pepper

Soak the beans overnight or use the quick-soak method (p. 165).
    Bring beans to boil, well covered with fresh salted water. Add boiling water as necessary to keep beans covered, while simmering until tender, for 2 to 3 hours. When beans are tender, remove from heat but do not drain. In a large, heavy casserole, heat the olive oil and sauté onions and pepper lightly. Add the

beef and cook until there is no trace of redness. Add the beans, the water in which they were cooked, and all other ingredients. Cover and simmer on lowest heat for 1 hour. Adjust seasoning before serving.

SERVES 8

Jane Flora's Chili

Jane and James Flora are great artists, great cooks, and great companions. James has illustrated recipes for many cookbooks, and Jane takes time out from her painting and sculpture to dish up feasts for fortunate friends.

    5 tablespoons lard or vegetable oil
    4 large onions, chopped
    2 cloves garlic, mashed
    2 pounds lean ground beef
    2 pounds lean ground pork
    Two 35-ounce cans tomatoes
    Two 12-ounce cans tomato paste
    1 teaspoon oregano
    1 generous teaspoon powdered cumin
    1 bay leaf
    3 cups pinto beans, cooked, or 2 cups leftover frijoles
    16 tortillas
    8 ounces Monterey Jack or cheddar cheese, grated
    4 whole scallions, cut into ½-inch lengths

In a large heavy skillet, heat 2 tablespoons of lard or oil and sauté onions and garlic until translucent. Add the beef and pork, breaking it up with a fork, and cook until all redness has disappeared. Add the tomatoes, tomato paste, oregano, cumin, bay leaf, and beans. Simmer partly covered for 2 or 3 hours, stirring occasionally.

Heat remaining 3 tablespoons lard or oil in a shallow skillet and dip tortillas into oil, one by one, for about 30 seconds each, until each tortilla is crisp. Drain separately on paper towels.

To serve, heap a plate with the chili and stick two freshly fried tortillas into the chili so they stand upright. Decorate each dish with a sprinkling of grated cheese, and a scattering of fresh green scallions.

SERVES 8

🎜 Mexicali Cornbread Chili

Not very authentic but, with a tankard of good Mexican beer on the side, a great feast for gringos.

      1 pound lean ground beef
      1 large onion, chopped
      4 cloves garlic, mashed
      2 tablespoons lard, oil, or bacon fat
      2 cups chopped tomatoes, fresh or canned
      ½ cup bran
      2 tablespoons chili powder
      ½ teaspoon oregano
      ½ teaspoon powdered cumin
      ½ teaspoon salt
      1 cup cornmeal
      1 egg
      1 cup milk or buttermilk
      1 tablespoon melted butter
      ½ teaspoon baking soda

Sauté meat, onion, and garlic in the fat until onion becomes translucent. Add tomatoes, bran, chili powder, oregano, cumin, and salt, cover, and simmer for 20 minutes.

Preheat oven to 400° F. Mix remaining ingredients and spread this crust over top of meat mixture, either in dumpling style or flat, as a piecrust. Bake for 30 minutes, or until crust turns golden brown.

SERVES 4

𝕏 Panhandle Chili

Another in the long line of chilies, authentic according to some-
one's chili philosophy. It's tasty and hearty, perfect for a cold
night.

    2 tablespoons lard or vegetable oil
    2 pounds boneless chuck steak, coarsely ground or
        cut into small cubes
    1 onion, diced
    2 cloves garlic, minced
    4 dried red peppers, seeded and chopped
    6-ounce can tomato paste
    1½ cups water
    1 tablespoon instant coffee
    1 tablespoon sugar
    1 tablespoon Hungarian paprika
    1 tablespoon oregano
    1 teaspoon salt
    1 teaspoon freshly ground black pepper
    1 teaspoon powdered cumin
    2 tablespoons masa harina or white cornmeal (optional)
    4 tablespoons finely minced onion
    4 tablespoons grated Monterey Jack cheese

Heat lard or oil in a large pot over a medium-high flame. Brown
meat with the onion and garlic. Lower heat to medium, and add
the red peppers, tomato paste, water, coffee, sugar, paprika,
oregano, salt, pepper, and cumin. Bring to boil, cover, and simmer for at least 1 hour.

The dish will be improved if you sprinkle it with 2 tablespoons masa harina or cornmeal and cook, stirring, for 5 minutes to thicken slightly.

Before serving sprinkle with the onion and cheese.

SERVES 6 TO 8

Pork

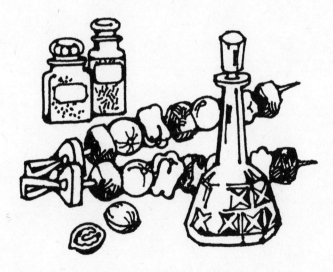

𝕽 Roast Pork, Jamaican-Style

This is a succulent and unusual roast.

> 4-pound loin of pork, with bone in
> freshly ground black pepper
> 1 teaspoon salt
> 1 teaspoon powdered ginger
> ½ teaspoon powdered cloves
> 2 cloves garlic, finely minced
> 1 cup dark Jamaican rum
> 2 cups chicken stock, as needed
> 2 bay leaves
> ½ cup brown sugar
> ⅓ cup lime juice
> 2 teaspoons cornstarch, mixed with 1 tablespoon water

Heat oven to 325° F. Score fat side of pork in a diamond pattern. Mix three grindings of the pepper, the salt, ginger, cloves, and garlic together in a small bowl, and rub well into the meat. Set the meat, fat side up, on a rack in a roasting pan. Combine ½ cup of the rum with ½ cup stock, and carefully pour it over the roast. Lay the bay leaves on top of the meat, and roast, allowing 30 minutes per pound. After 1 hour, baste with a sauce made of the brown sugar, lime juice, and remaining ½ cup rum. Continue to baste the roast with juices occasionally, adding more stock to the pan if necessary. When roast is done, discard bay leaves, set meat on a platter, and keep warm. Drain excess fat from roasting pan, and place pan on burner over medium flame. Bring liquid up to 2 cups by adding stock and any remaining basting sauce. Bring to a boil, then add cornstarch mixture. Stir constantly until gravy thickens. Adjust seasonings to taste and serve gravy to accompany roast.

SERVES 6 TO 8

Hungarian Potted Pork

Hungarians love their spices. *I* love the flavor juniper berries give a dish. This delicious, sturdy dinner treat must have been created with them and me in mind.

1 tablespoon bacon fat
5-pound boneless loin of pork
2 carrots, thinly sliced
2 small parsnips, thinly sliced
2 small bell peppers, thinly sliced
2 small tomatoes, chopped
1 cup red wine
1 tablespoon Hungarian paprika
2 tablespoons lemon juice
1 bay leaf
6 juniper berries, bruised
salt and freshly ground black pepper to taste

Preheat over to 350° F. In a flameproof casserole, heat the bacon fat over medium-high flame. Add the pork loin, and sauté, turning it frequently, until golden brown, about 15 minutes. Add all remaining ingredients, cover, and roast in oven for about 3 hours, until done. Remove meat to warm platter, and slice it. Press vegetables and sauce through a sieve and pour over meat.

SERVES 6 TO 8

🦋 Masai's Oriental Pork

Masai was a Japanese girl who made her own American version
of this Chinese dish. When I first tasted this excellent preparation, it was served not only with steamed rice but with rounds
of hot well-buttered caraway rye bread dotted with short scallion
lengths, plus a tart green salad. Amazingly enough, with chilled
German beer on the side, it all worked. The spicy-minded will
want Chinese mustard as an accompaniment.

¾ cup soy sauce
½ cup white vinegar
2 tablespoons dry mustard
½ cup sugar
¼ teaspoon Chinese Five-Spice Powder (optional; p. 11)
3½-pound boneless loin of pork
2 cups long-grain rice, steamed (p. 168)

In an ovenproof dish make marinade by blending the soy, vinegar, mustard, sugar, and optional spice powder. Set the meat
in the marinade and let stand for at least 1 hour, turning meat
several times to coat well.

Preheat oven to 450° F. Place meat in oven, and as soon
as liquid boils, turn oven down to 350° F. and let it cook for
1½ hours. Baste every 15 minutes until sauce finally becomes
thick, about an hour, then baste every 5 minutes. However, if
sauce fails to thicken, don't worry; it will develop a good consistency as it cools during serving.

To serve, remove meat from sauce and put sauce in a gravy
boat. Slice meat thinly and serve on top of a bed of dry steamed
rice. Each guest spoons on as much of the piquant sauce as he or
she wishes.

SERVES 4 TO 6

ℵ Spicy Barbecued Pork

This is a wonderful dish from Marjorie Thorson Parsons, who, as
a busy person, tries to cook well in the least possible time, with
the least possible fuss. The results of this dish will belie its simple origins.

> 4-pound boneless loin of pork
> ⅓ cup dark molasses
> ⅓ cup soy sauce
> ⅓ cup Dijon mustard
> ¼ cup white vinegar
> 2 tablespoons Worcestershire sauce
> 2 teaspoons Tabasco
> 2 cups long-grain rice, steamed (p. 168)

Trim all fat from pork, and marinate in a sauce made by mixing
remaining ingredients except the rice. Marinate for 2 hours if
there is time; if not, throw it right in the oven and it will turn out
fine. Roast at 350° F. for 2 to 2½ hours, until pork is done. Baste
frequently. When the sauce becomes thick and glazes the meat,
any fat left will have separated from it. Pour off the fat. Should
the meat become too glazed before it is ready, add a tiny bit of
water to the sauce. Serve with rice.

Any leftover sauce will keep indefinitely in the refrigerator.

SERVES 6

ℵ Carne de Vinha d'Alhos
Pickled Pork

Hawaii is one of the world's great melting pots. No matter that
the national dish, maui maui (dolphin) has to be shipped over
frozen from Los Angeles. No matter that tourists' tastes dictate a
steak-and-potatoes thinking in most of the islands' restaurants.
Go behind the commercialized hula shows and you'll find hide-
away Korean, Japanese, Polynesian, and Portuguese eating
places. Memories of Portugal inspired this tasty Hawaiian dish.

1½ pounds lean boneless pork, cut into 1-inch cubes
1½ cups white vinegar
2 cloves garlic
6 dried red peppers, seeded
1 bay leaf
2 teaspoons salt
6 whole cloves
¼ teaspoon thyme
¼ teaspoon sage
2 teaspoons peanut oil
2 potatoes, peeled and thinly sliced, or 6 slices
    stale bread (optional)

Combine all ingredients except peanut oil and potatoes or bread. Cover and refrigerate for at least 2 days, turning meat daily. When ready to cook, simmer pork in the marinating liquid for 25 minutes. Drain pork and fry over medium-low heat in peanut oil for 25 minutes more, or until meat is well done.

If desired, reserve pork and fry sliced potatoes, or slices of bread, in the same fat until they are brown. Serve all together.

SERVES 4 TO 6

🎜 Portuguese Pork with Cumin

A splendid Portuguese recipe that—unlike many—does not feature codfish. This makes a fine, oddly subtle stew.

4 pounds lean boneless pork, cut into 1-inch cubes
2 cups dry white wine
1 bay leaf
1 teaspoon Hungarian paprika
3 cloves garlic, minced
¼ teaspoon powdered cloves
1 teaspoon cumin seed, crushed
2 tablespoons diced salt pork
2 teaspoons salt
2 cups water
4 potatoes, peeled and cubed (optional)
¼ cup white port or light brandy

Marinate the meat at least 24 hours in the dry white wine, bay leaf, paprika, and garlic. Remove meat from marinade and rub with mixture of cloves and cumin. Reserve 1 cup of marinade. In a large, heavy pot, render the salt pork. When it has browned, add the pork cubes and brown over high heat. Sprinkle with salt, and add 1 cup of the marinade and 2 cups of water. Cover and simmer for about 1 hour, until meat is quite tender. Potatoes can be added during the last half hour, if desired. Just before serving, add the port or brandy.

SERVES 6

Mee Krob
Rice Noodles Thai-Style

One of the tantalizing standards in the Thai cuisine, Mee Krob is genuinely spicy and genuinely delicious. It is well worth the effort of seeking out the rice noodles and the yellow bean paste that make the dish unique. Any Chinese market will have them, or see Mail-Order Sources.

> 4 cups peanut oil
> 2 eggs
> ½ pound rice noodles
> 3 cloves garlic, finely chopped
> 1 small onion, finely chopped
> 1 pound lean boneless pork, cut into ½-inch cubes
> ¼ cup yellow bean paste
> 2 tablespoons catsup
> ¾ cup sugar
> ¼ cup soy sauce
> ½ cup lemon juice
> 1 tablespoon lemon peel, minced
> ½ pound bean sprouts, washed
> 2 fresh hot red peppers, seeded and minced
> 2 whole scallions, cut into 1-inch pieces

Pour the oil into a wok or deep pot heated over a high flame. Beat eggs thoroughly, and trickle them by the spoonful in a lace-like pattern into heated oil. Quickly remove egg lace with slotted spoon to dry on paper towels. Next, brown the rice noodles quickly in the oil—about 15 seconds to a side. Carefully dry noodles between paper towels.

Pour off all but ¼ cup of oil and add the garlic and onion. Stir-fry for 1 minute, then add the pork cubes, bean paste, and catsup. Bring to a boil, then stir in the sugar. At glassy syrup stage, add the soy sauce, reduce heat, and simmer uncovered until liquid is very thick (about 10 minutes). Stir in lemon juice and lemon peel and cook 4 minutes more.

Pile the rice noodles on a heated platter, add about ½ cup of sauce, and mix *lightly*. Build up, using ½ cup sauce at a time. Top the platter with layers of egg lace, then with the bean sprouts. Garnish with the peppers and scallions, either over the top or on the side.

SERVES 4

Indonesian Saté

Saté is a classic Indonesian and Malaysian dish with many variations. This one is a composite I put together, combining the best features of several different recipes. It does not have to be served with the hot peanut butter sauce, but without it you lose half the distinctiveness of the dish. Saté is best cooked over charcoal and served with plain rice, Chinese fried rice, or Bahmi Goreng (following recipe).

10 walnuts, grated
2 tablespoons coriander seed, crushed
3 cloves garlic, minced
1 teaspoon dried red pepper flakes
4 onions, grated
1 cup fresh orange juice
juice of 1 lemon
2 tablespoons brown sugar
3 tablespoons soy sauce
2 pounds lean boneless pork, cut into 1½-inch cubes
Hot Peanut Butter Sauce (p. 241)

In a large bowl, mix well all ingredients except meat and peanut butter sauce. Add the pork, turning and pressing the mixture into the meat. Marinate in refrigerator for at least 2 hours.
Thread meat on skewers and broil over charcoal, or in oven, for
about 15 to 20 minutes, or until done, turning to brown all sides.
Serve with peanut butter sauce.

SERVES 6

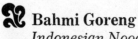 Bahmi Goreng
Indonesian Noodle Dish

Nasi goreng (a fried rice dish) and bahmi goreng (noodle dish)
are two inevitable classics at any 21-Boy *Rijstaffel*. *Rijstaffel*
means "rice table," a feast favored by the Dutch, who brought
it home from colonial Indonesia. It is a whopping meal, but less
whopping than the Indonesian original. After sipping jenever
(Dutch gin), colonials would retire to the table, and fill a large
soup bowl with steamed rice. Then a parade of twenty-one "boys"
would march past, each bearing a meat dish, a fiery condiment,
a sweet fruit, vegetables, and pickles, along with salted peanuts
and almonds. Classically, there would be an empty side plate on
which each feaster would line up his choices, to be mixed in
varying combinations with the rice. (Only a neophyte would mix
the *rijstaffel* together on top of his rice.) Great quantities of
chilled beer were consumed to wash down the highly spiced
foods.

The following recipe is not as difficult to make as it may
look, and it is very good.

1½ pounds lean boneless pork
½ pound fine Chinese egg noodles (or vermicelli)
⅓ cup plus 2 tablespoons soy sauce
2 cloves garlic, mashed
6 whole scallions, chopped
2 eggs
9 tablespoons peanut oil
2 large onions, thinly sliced
1 thin slice fresh ginger, minced
3 cups chopped Chinese or celery cabbage
1½ cups small shrimp, shelled and cooked
1 cup bean sprouts
freshly ground black pepper

Julienne the pork: cut into strips about 2 inches long, ⅛ inch wide and thick.

Cook the noodles in boiling water for about 3 minutes. Drain, spread thinly on a large plate, and chill in refrigerator.

Combine ⅓ cup soy sauce with the garlic and scallions, and marinate pork strips in the mixture for 2 hours, stirring occasionally.

Beat eggs thoroughly, and spread very thinly in a heated, lightly oiled skillet. Cook until set and slide out onto a large plate. Cool and cut into thin ribbons.

To prepare the dish, heat 2 tablespoons of the oil over high flame in a wok or iron skillet. Add pork, including marinade, and sauté for 3 minutes, or until pork is cooked. Remove to a plate. Heat 2 more tablespoons of the oil in a wok and add onions and ginger. Sauté until onions are limp. Remove to a plate.

Heat 2 more tablespoons of the oil, and sauté cabbage and shrimp for 3 minutes. Return pork, onions, and ginger to mixture, and stir in 2 tablespoons soy sauce. Season to taste with freshly ground pepper. Lower heat, and let simmer 3 minutes. Toss in the bean sprouts.

In another skillet, heat 3 tablespoons oil over medium-high flame. Add the chilled noodles and stir-fry until crisp and partly browned. Remove noodles from oil, place on a warm platter, and pour the pork-shrimp mixture over them. Garnish with egg strips, and serve immediately.

SERVES 4 TO 6

❧ Cheong's Twice-Cooked Pork

Cheong's Garden, in West Hempstead, New York, is one of my favorite restaurants. Owner Francis Cheong, who knows nearly everything there is to know about the Chinese kitchen, graciously gave me two classic recipes for inclusion in this book. Follow the directions carefully, and you can't go wrong. Preserved bean curd, bok choy, and hoisin sauce are available in Chinese markets, or see Mail-Order Sources. Serve the dish with rice.

1½ pounds lean boneless pork
1 large bell pepper, seeded
3 cups chopped bok choy (Chinese cabbage)
6 to 8 pieces preserved bean curd
4 teaspoons heavy soy sauce, or 6 tablespoons regular
   soy sauce
1 teaspoon dry sherry
3 tablespoons hoisin sauce
½ teaspoon sesame oil
2 teaspoons cornstarch
½ teaspoon salt
freshly ground black pepper to taste
2 tablespoons water
6 tablespoons peanut oil
4 whole scallions, minced
1 teaspoon powdered Szechuan chili or dried red pepper
   flakes
4 cloves garlic, minced
2 tablespoons minced fresh ginger

Simmer pork for 30 minutes in water to cover. Meanwhile, cut bell pepper into 1-inch squares and place in large bowl. Cut bok choy into pieces 2½ inches long, 1 inch wide, and add to bowl. Cut bean curd in half, then into ¼-inch slices; add to bowl, and set aside.

In a separate bowl, blend soy sauce, sherry, hoisin sauce, sesame oil, cornstarch, salt, and pepper. Add water, and mix thoroughly to form a smooth sauce. Set aside.

Drain and cool pork, and cut it into small, thin slices (2½ by 1 by ¼ inch).

Heat peanut oil over high flame in a wok or large iron skillet. Add scallions, powdered chili or pepper flakes, garlic, and ginger. After 5 seconds, add pork slices and bowl of vegetables. Stir-fry for 1 minute. Add sauce, and stir-fry for 1 minute more. Pour into serving bowl, and serve immediately.

SERVES 4

 Korean Pork Strips

Typical of the Oriental cuisines, these barbecued strips are equally suitable for a cocktail party or as part of a Korean or Chinese meal. This recipe calls for Five-Spice Powder, which is an indispensable Chinese seasoning mix. You can purchase it in an Oriental market, or make your own (p. 11).

1 clove garlic, mashed
½ teaspoon Five-Spice Powder
½ teaspoon sesame seed
½ cup sherry
1 pound lean boneless pork, cut into finger-length strips

Mix all ingredients except pork to make a marinade. Steep the pork strips in it for several hours, or overnight. Remove pork from liquid and broil in oven or over charcoal, basting with marinade, until meat is cooked through and golden brown on both sides.

SERVES 4 TO 6

West Indies Garlic Pork

Originally from Portugal, this unusual dish can be served with a hot Creole sauce as an appetizer with cocktails, or with rice or sweet potatoes as a main course. This goes well with West Indies Dip Sauce (p. 236) or any similar sauce.

6 cloves garlic, chopped
1 fresh hot red pepper, seeded and chopped
1 teaspoon chopped fresh marjoram or thyme
2 teaspoons salt
generous grinding black pepper
juice of 1 large lime
2 cups white vinegar
3 pounds lean boneless pork, cut into 1-inch cubes
4 tablespoons oil or lard

Put the chopped garlic, red pepper, marjoram or thyme, salt, and pepper in a jar with a tight-fitting lid. Add the lime juice and vinegar. Shake well to mix. Place pork cubes in a bowl, and pour mixture over them. Marinate in refrigerator for 2 days, turning meat occasionally. Drain and pat dry with paper towels. In a skillet, heat oil or lard just short of smoking. Stir-fry pork until done (about 15 minutes).

SERVES 6 AS A MAIN DISH,
12 TO 16 AS APPETIZER

Pork Chops à la Charcutière

Pork chops "in the style of the pork butcher" are to be found, proudly prepared by said butcher, in most cities and towns of France. In restaurants, the preparation is apt to be more ambitious. In essence, the dish is made from breaded pork chops, served with a charcutière sauce. This is a sauce Robert (an oniony glazed white wine sauce), which is spiced with mustard and strengthened with a julienne of gherkins. I have found this simplified American version almost equal to the original. If you end up with more sauce than you need, save it. It goes beautifully with almost any meat or poultry dish. For an echo of the classic dish, make a mound of soft mashed potatoes, stand each chop erect around the potato mountain, and bring the dish hot to the table.

    salt and freshly ground black pepper
    six 2-inch-thick pork chops
    3 tablespoons butter
    1 onion, finely chopped
    1 tablespoon black peppercorns, crushed
    ½ cup red wine vinegar
    2 small tomatoes, peeled and finely chopped
    2 tablespoons tomato purée
    1 cup brown gravy or rich stock
    1 tablespoon chopped fresh parsley
    ½ teaspoon thyme
    ½ teaspoon tarragon
    ½ cup water
    2 tablespoons Dijon mustard

Lightly salt the chops, rub in a few grinds of pepper, and sauté them in 1 tablespoon of the butter. Cook for 15 minutes or more on each side, until browned and thoroughly done. Remove the chops and keep them warm in a serving dish. Pour off fat but reserve skillet for later.

In another pan, sauté the onion in 1 tablespoon of the butter for 2 minutes. Add the crushed peppercorns and ¼ cup vinegar. Reduce until most of the vinegar has evaporated. Add the chopped tomatoes and simmer until slightly thick. Add the to-mato purée, the gravy or stock, parsley, thyme, tarragon, and water. Salt to taste, and simmer for 10 minutes. Keep warm, but do not boil.

Set the pork chop skillet over a low flame and add remain-ing ¼ cup vinegar. Scrape with a wooden spoon to dissolve all brown particles.

Add this vinegar mixture to the other pan and mix well. Add the mustard and remaining tablespoon of butter. Stir, but do not cook further. Pass the sauce to be spooned over the pork chops.

SERVES 6

ℵ Pork Chops in Mustard Cream

A little rich, a little piquant, a little divine.

    six 1-inch-thick loin pork chops
    ½ cup white wine or dry Vermouth
    ½ cup flour
    salt and freshly ground black pepper
    ¼ cup oil
    ½ teaspoon crumbled sage
    ½ teaspoon thyme
    3 cloves garlic, halved
    4 tablespoons butter
    2 cups heavy cream
    1 tablespoon dry mustard
    2 tablespoons tomato purée
    1 small bunch watercress, chopped

Place chops in baking dish and cover with the wine. Marinate for 1 hour. Preheat oven to 300° F. Remove chops from marinade and dredge lightly with flour. Season lightly with salt and pepper.

In a large iron skillet heat the oil and brown the chops over high heat, about 4 minutes to a side. Return chops to the baking dish, and dust with sage and thyme. Sauté garlic in butter, but do not brown. Pour this over the meat.

Cover the chops and bake 1 hour, basting frequently.

Meanwhile, reduce the cream in a saucepan over low heat to ⅔ cup. Combine mustard and tomato purée in a bowl, and whisk, gradually adding the reduced cream. When well beaten, spoon this sauce over the chops and reduce oven heat to 250° F. Cover and bake 20 minutes longer. Garnish with chopped watercress and serve hot.

SERVES 6

Lamb

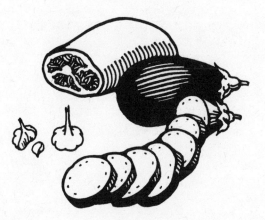

ಔ Roast Lamb, Muslim-Style

No one can match the Middle Easterners when it comes to doing justice to lamb. The Muslims of this recipe seem to have originated in India, judging by the selection of spices used.

2 tablespoons grated fresh ginger
5 cloves garlic, mashed
½ cup yogurt
1½ teaspoons salt
freshly ground black pepper
juice of 1 lime
4- to 5-pound leg of lamb
1 tablespoon powdered coriander
½ teaspoon cayenne
½ teaspoon powdered cloves
½ teaspoon powdered cinnamon
½ teaspoon powdered cardamom

Mix ginger, garlic, yogurt, salt, a generous grinding of pepper, and lime juice. Cut small gashes in the lamb and rub the yogurt mixture well into the meat. Let stand for at least 2 hours.

Heat oven to 350° F. Combine remaining ingredients in a skillet, and stir over low heat for 2 minutes. Cool. Sprinkle the spices over the lamb and roast for 2 hours.

SERVES 6 TO 8

𝒩 Hungarian Gulyás with Little Dumplings

A gulyás (or goulash, or goulasch) is the Hungarian "herdsman's meat." For all the variations, it is basically a meat stew seasoned with paprika. This one is spicy, and I suggest lamb, though beef is fine, too.

> 1 tablespoon lard or butter
> 3 pounds boneless stewing lamb or beef, cut into
>   1-inch cubes
> 1 large onion, minced
> 1 tablespoon hot Hungarian paprika, or 1 tablespoon
>   paprika and a good dash of cayenne
> ½ cup water
> ¼ teaspoon caraway seed
> 2 cloves garlic, mashed
> 1 teaspoon salt
> 4 medium potatoes, diced
> 2 bell peppers, seeded and diced
> 2 tomatoes, diced
> ½ cup stock or broth, or more as needed
> Hungarian-Style Little Dumplings (p. 257)

In a heavy kettle, melt lard or butter over medium flame and brown meat and onion lightly. Remove from heat and at once stir in paprika, plus water. Add caraway seed, garlic, and salt. Return to stove and cook, covered, over very low heat for about 2 hours, or until meat is tender. Add potatoes, peppers, tomatoes, and stock or broth. Simmer, covered, for about 30 minutes. (If liquid gets low, add more stock, or a little water.) Prepare the dumplings and add to broth.

SERVES 6 TO 8

🎜 Persian Lamb and Eggplant Stew

For the authentic Persian touch, add a handful of dried apricots to this dish in the last hour's cooking. Serve with fresh spinach salad and yogurt.

        1 plump eggplant
        salt
        ½ cup olive oil
        2 large onions, thinly sliced
        2 pounds boneless stewing lamb, cut into 1-inch cubes
        3 tomatoes, peeled and chopped, or 28-ounce can
            tomatoes, drained and chopped
        juice of 1 lemon
        1 teaspoon powdered cinnamon, or 1 whole stick
        ½ teaspoon freshly grated nutmeg
        freshly ground black pepper
        ½ cup water
        6 dried apricots (optional)

Rinse eggplant and pat it dry. Trim the ends, but do not peel it. Cut into 1-inch cubes and place them in a colander. Salt lightly, and let drain for 30 minutes. Pat dry. In a skillet, heat about ¼ cup oil and sauté the eggplant pieces a few at a time. When they are tender and translucent, remove them to a plate. Add the rest of the oil and sauté the onions until translucent. Add the lamb and stir until meat is brown on all sides. Cover and simmer for 20 minutes. Add remaining ingredients. Cover and cook slowly for about 1 hour, checking occasionally to see if more water is required.

SERVES 6

🎜 Fasoulya
Armenian Green Bean Stew

One of the first Middle Eastern dishes I ever tasted, and still one of the best. The sauce is wonderful for dipping, so I long ago

Americanized the dish by accompanying it with warmed slices of
crusty French bread—sourdough, if available. Fasoulya comes
in as many versions as there are Armenian households; this is a
good one from California. It makes a superb one-dish meal for,
say, a folk dance or poker group. Hearty and tangy, its simplicity doesn't let it get in the way of the major action. Lamb is
the traditional meat, of course, but beef is fine.

> 2 tablespoons butter
> 2 onions, chopped
> 1 pound ground lamb
> 1½ pounds fresh green beans, coarsely chopped, or two
>   10-ounce packages frozen green beans
> 4 tomatoes, peeled, seeded, and coarsely chopped, or
>   35-ounce can tomatoes, drained and coarsely chopped
> 2 cloves garlic, finely chopped
> ¼ teaspoon cayenne
> ½ teaspoon salt
> 1 cup water

In a large heavy saucepan, melt butter over medium heat and
sauté onions until golden. Add meat, breaking it up with a fork,
and cook until it has lost its redness. Add remaining ingredients,
and stir to mix. Cover and simmer until beans are tender (about
40 minutes for fresh beans; 20 minutes for frozen).

SERVES 4

 ## Kibbi
Middle Eastern Meat Pie

Kibbi, when made of the finest lamb, is often eaten raw. I prefer it cooked as a kind of "pie." Kibbi can also be made into meatballs and charcoal-broiled. In that case, serve the meatballs
warm in a little tomato sauce. The tasty cracked wheat is known
variously throughout the Middle East as burghul, bulgur, bulghur,
or bulgour. The dish goes well with a pilaf and stewed okra or
any green vegetable.

Lining

2½ cups fine bulgur
2 pounds lean ground lamb
1 small onion, grated
1 teaspoon salt
freshly ground black pepper
¼ teaspoon powdered cinnamon

Filling

1 tablespoon butter
2 onions, chopped
½ pound ground lamb with a little fat in it
¼ cup pine nuts
½ teaspoon salt
freshly ground black pepper

2 tablespoons butter for glazing

This kibbi is a meat loaf in three layers.

To make the lining, rinse the bulgur in a colander and empty into a pan to soak in water for 15 minutes. Drain bulgur and mix it well with the 2 pounds of lamb, the grated onion, and the salt, pepper, and cinnamon. Knead to mix thoroughly.

To make the filling, heat 1 tablespoon butter, and fry the 2 chopped onions until golden. Add the ½ pound lamb and stir until it loses color. Add the pine nuts and the salt and pepper.

Press half the lining mixture into a greased 9-by-12-inch baking pan. Add the filling. Top with the rest of the lining mixture, press down firmly, and cut diamond-shaped patterns in the top. Dot top with butter. Bake at 400° F. for 30 minutes. Reduce heat to 300° F. and bake 30 minutes longer.

SERVES 8

Ham,
Sausages,
& Mixed
Meats

🙝 Ham Loaf

An early American dish, perfected long ago by a great California cook, Helen Roberts. The sassy dish goes beautifully with a crisp green salad, green peas, and scalloped potatoes.

2 pounds ground pork
1 pound ground smoked ham
1 cup milk
1 cup bread crumbs
2 eggs, lightly beaten
salt and freshly ground black pepper to taste
1 cup brown sugar
½ cup water
½ cup white wine vinegar
¼ cup catsup
1 teaspoon dry mustard

Thoroughly mix the pork, ham, milk, bread crumbs, eggs, salt, and pepper and shape into a loaf that will just fit a 9-by-12-inch baking pan. Mix remaining ingredients, punch holes in loaf, and pour the mixture over it. Bake 1½ hours at 350° F., basting every 15 minutes.

SERVES 6 TO 8

℔ Home-Style Sage Sausage

Not many people serve homemade sausage these days, and that's a pity. Perhaps this easy-to-make recipe will start the sausages rolling again.

> 1 pound lean ground pork
> 2 tablespoons crumbled dried or fresh sage leaves
> 1 tablespoon crumbled marjoram
> 1 teaspoon salt
> 1 teaspoon freshly grated nutmeg
> ¼ teaspoon powdered coriander
> ⅛ teaspoon cayenne
> ⅛ teaspoon powdered cloves

In a large bowl, blend all ingredients together thoroughly. Let rest for 30 minutes for flavors to blend. Shape into thin patties, and cook in a skillet over low heat until well done.

SERVES 4 TO 6

℔ Homemade Sausage, Indian-Style

This is a recipe a British housewife living in India might have put together. The spices can be adjusted to your own taste. Experiment, make notes, and play: that's what a recipe is for.

> 1½ pounds lean pork
> 1 teaspoon coriander seed
> generous dash powdered cinnamon
> generous dash powdered cloves
> dash freshly grated nutmeg
> 1 teaspoon salt
> 1 or 2 tablespoons white vinegar, as needed

Have your butcher coarsely grind the lean pork, or pass it through your own meat grinder. Mash the coriander seed in a mortar, and toast in dry skillet over low heat until lightly colored. Add coriander, cinnamon, cloves, nutmeg, and salt to the pork. Mix well. Moisten the mixture with vinegar until soft, manageable patties can be formed. Let set for 30 minutes for flavors to blend. Make patties about ½ inch thick.

Sauté the patties over low heat until brown on both sides, turning just once.

MAKES 6 TO 8 PATTIES

🎵 Homemade Chorizo

Chorizo is to Mexicans what salami is to Italians and linguisa is to the Portuguese, or what a good smoked pork sausage was to an early American farmer. Never mind the casing; make patties.

    1 pound coarsely ground lean pork
    1 teaspoon salt
    2 tablespoons chili powder
    1 clove garlic, mashed
    1 teaspoon oregano, hand-rubbed
    2 tablespoons vinegar

Thoroughly mix pork with all other ingredients. Let meld for 30 minutes in the refrigerator.

When ready to cook, shape into thin patties and sauté gently until both sides are golden brown, about 10 minutes to each side.

Uncooked, the sausage will keep for a week in refrigerator in a tightly sealed jar.

MAKES 1 POUND SAUSAGE

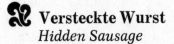 Spicy Sicilian Cheese Sausage

A hearty peasant sausage, this is also excellent as a spicy stuffing for poultry.

3 pounds freshly ground lean pork
1½ pounds freshly ground beef
1½ cups minced fresh flat-leaf parsley
¾ cup coarsely grated Romano cheese
¼ cup coarsely grated Parmesan cheese
3 tablespoons fennel seed
5 teaspoons salt
freshly ground black pepper (about 10 grindings)
dash cayenne

Combine meats with parsley and remaining ingredients; mix well. If needed, add a little water so that ingredients are lightly bound together. Shape sausage into small flat rounds and cook in a skillet over low heat until crusty and cooked through, about 10 minutes to a side.

MAKES ABOUT 5 POUNDS

Versteckte Wurst
Hidden Sausage

A hearty and flexible dish from Germany, best made to your own proportions. Try these quantities the first time, then adjust to your taste. The sausage should be the spiciest you can find.

1 pound spicy link sausage
2 tablespoons vegetable oil
1 pound sauerkraut
2 onions, thinly sliced
½ teaspoon caraway seed
4 cups mashed cooked potatoes

Heat oven to 350° F. Cut the sausage into ⅓-inch slices, lay them flat in a large skillet, and cook over low heat until done, about 15 minutes, turning them once. Remove sausage from skillet and place on paper to drain. Add the oil to the skillet, heat, and add sauerkraut, onions, and caraway seed. Sauté over medium heat until the onions are tender, stirring occasionally.

In a flat baking dish, alternate layers of sausage with layers of the sauerkraut mixture. Cover with the mashed potatoes, and bake for 15 minutes, or until top is browned.

SERVES 4

 **Lapin à la Moutarde**
Rabbit in Mustard

Rabbit is not much eaten in this country, which is a pity. As this recipe proves, it makes a delicious dish. (Of course, you may substitute chicken.)

    3 tablespoons Dijon mustard
    2 tablespoons fresh bread crumbs
    1 tablespoon olive oil
    1 rabbit (or 1 fryer), cut into serving-size pieces
    1 cup dry white wine
    1 cup light cream
    salt and freshly ground black pepper to taste

Heat oven to 400° F. Make a paste of the mustard, crumbs, and oil. Spread this over all the meat. Put the meat in a roasting pan and add the white wine. Roast until meat is tender but not dry (about 45 minutes). Remove meat from oven and place on warm platter. Place roasting pan over high heat on stove top. Add the cream, salt, and pepper to the pan. Bring to a boil, stirring constantly, and boil for about 2 minutes. Pour over the meat and serve at once.

SERVES 4

𝕭 Hare Braised with Juniper Berries

Here is another delicious recipe for rabbit. This one is Hungarian.
Chicken or lamb may be substituted. Serve with noodles.

    6 juniper berries, crushed
    ½ teaspoon salt
    2 pounds hare or chicken, cut up, or 2 pounds boned,
        cubed leg of lamb
    1 onion, minced
    2 tablespoons flour
    ¼ pound bacon, cut into small pieces
    ¼ cup red wine or water
    1 cup sour cream
    salt and freshly ground black pepper

Crush the berries in the salt and rub them into the meat. Cover
meat and refrigerate for 2 days. When ready to cook, sprinkle
meat with minced onion, and dust with the flour.

Brown the meat and onion in a skillet with the bacon, then
sprinkle it with the wine or water. Shake the pan, cover, and
cook over low heat for about 45 minutes. Peek and add more
liquid if it has all evaporated. Remove meat when tender, and
keep it warm. Pour off surplus fat from skillet.

Strain the broth. Add sour cream and simmer, without boiling, for a few minutes. Add salt and a generous grinding of
pepper to taste, and pour sauce over meat.

SERVES 6 TO 8

𝕭 Couscous

All across North Africa couscous is a prized dish, and it is the
national dish of Morocco. A seafood variant is to be found in
Sicily, where they called it *cuscusu*. Properly, you make couscous in a couscousière—but you can improvise with a large colander suspended over a large pot. Place a kitchen towel over the

colander, and top it with a lid to keep all the steam in. Following is one of the simpler recipes. If you have any favorite vegetables, toss them in. You can buy couscous in packages in Middle Eastern stores. If you don't tell your neighbors, you can substitute bulgur or kasha or any brown cereal. Be as generous as you dare with the hot pepper, as this is traditionally an exceptionally spicy dish.

¼ cup chickpeas
1 pound couscous
2 pounds boneless leg of lamb, cubed, or 1 pound
 lamb and 1 pound chicken meat, cubed
2 carrots, coarsely chopped
1 onion, quartered
3 bay leaves
4 tablespoons tomato purée
3 teaspoons salt
1½ teaspoons dried red pepper flakes
2 teaspoons powdered cumin
1 teaspoon powdered ginger
½ teaspoon powdered cinnamon
4 tablespoons olive oil
8 stalks celery, coarsely chopped

Choice of several or all of the following:
2 turnips, peeled and chopped
1 yam, peeled and chopped
2 zucchini, chopped
2 eggplants, chopped
2 bell peppers, seeded and chopped
¼ cup raisins
2 tablespoons butter

bowl of harissa (p. 244)

Soak the chickpeas overnight. The next day, drain them, put them in a pan, and cover well with fresh water. Boil for about 1½ hours or until almost tender. Drain and set aside.

Empty the couscous onto a cookie sheet. Sprinkle with warm

water and work it with your fingers so that each grain begins to swell and becomes separate. Let couscous rest for 15 minutes. Repeat the process enough times so that all the grains become moist and separate.

Put the chickpeas in the bottom of a soup kettle or couscousière. Add the meat, carrots, and onion. Cover with water and bring to a boil. Reduce heat, cover, and simmer for 20 minutes.

Now add the bay leaves, tomato purée, salt, red pepper flakes, cumin, ginger, cinnamon, oil, celery, and turnips and yam, if used. Put the couscous in the upper part of the steamer and set over the lower part. (Make sure the liquid level in the lower pot is below the couscous.) Cover well, and use a towel if necessary to seal up any leaks between the two pots, so all the vapors pass up through the grain. Simmer, covered well, for 15 minutes.

Add the zucchini, eggplants, bell peppers, and raisins to the stew. Drop the butter into the couscous and re-cover tightly. Simmer another 15 minutes—or until all vegetables are *just tender*. Do not overcook.

To serve. Stir the couscous lightly with a fork to distribute the butter. Spread the couscous on a large warm platter. Make a well in the center and spoon in the vegetables and meat and some of the sauce. Serve the harissa on the side so each guest can make his couscous as spicy as he likes. Also serve the rest of the stew sauce as a side dish.

SERVES 6 TO 8

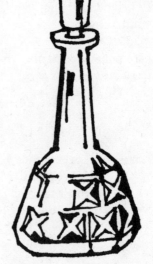

ℵ Kofta Curry
Curried Meatballs, Indian-Style

Kofta means "ball," and is spelled variously in different cuisines. Koftas, although easy to make, are quite exotic. Rice is the side dish.

> 1 pound ground lamb or beef
> 2 eggs
> ¼ teaspoon powdered cinnamon
> ¼ teaspoon powdered cloves
> ¼ teaspoon cayenne
> 1 scant teaspoon flour (optional)
> 5 tablespoons butter
> 1 teaspoon salt
> 1 large onion, sliced in thin rounds
> 1 rounded tablespoon curry powder (p. 13)
> 6-ounce can tomato paste
> 1½ cups boiling water
> cilantro (fresh coriander), chopped, for garnish

Mix the ground meat with the eggs, cinnamon, cloves, and cayenne—bind with a bit of flour if necessary. Make golf-ball shapes. Fry in 3 tablespoons of the butter until brown on all sides. Salt lightly. Keep warm.

In an iron skillet, heat remaining 2 tablespoons butter and sauté onion until browned. Add the curry powder and heat a minute or two. Add the tomato paste and the boiling water. Simmer 15 minutes. Add the meatballs, garnish with the cilantro, and serve hot.

SERVES 4

ℵ Creole Jambalaya

A typical Creole dish, jambalaya has as many definitions as there are smoky fireplaces in the Delta. This is an authentic version— make it once, then take off from there with chicken, squirrel, woodchuck, or any favorite meat as a base.

2 tablespoons butter
2 onions, chopped
2 bell peppers, seeded and chopped
3 whole scallions, thinly sliced
3 cloves garlic, minced
1 pound lean boneless pork, cubed
1 cup finely chopped baked ham
6 links smoked sausage, cut into ¼-inch slices
2 teaspoons salt
freshly ground black pepper to taste
dash cayenne
1 teaspoon good chili powder
2 bay leaves, crushed
pinch thyme
3 whole cloves, crushed
3 cups rich beef or chicken stock
1½ cups long-grain rice

Melt butter over medium heat in a large, heavy pot. Add the onions, bell peppers, scallions, and garlic. Stir, and add pork and ham. Sauté over low heat for about 15 minutes, stirring occasionally, until meat is browned. Add sausage slices, and all seasonings. Sauté for 5 minutes more. Add the stock, stir, then add the rice. Bring to a boil, turn heat to very low, and cover pot with a tight-fitting lid. Simmer for about 20 minutes. With a fork, gently fluff rice, lifting from the bottom. Serve while piping hot.

SERVES 6

 Babotee
South African Curry Custard

One might call this a South African moussaka. In any event, it is a delicious dish. The rice is necessary and the chutneys give élan. A Bengal Club chutney is good; or try Mango Chutney (see recipe).

1 onion, chopped
4 tablespoons butter
1½ pounds chopped cooked meat (beef, chicken, lamb)
1 slice bread soaked in white wine, then crumbled
juice of 1 lemon
peel of ½ lemon, grated
1 tablespoon curry powder (p. 13)
½ cup slivered blanched almonds
salt and freshly ground black pepper to taste
2 eggs
1 cup milk, scalded
1 bay leaf
2 cups cooked steamed rice
chutneys of choice

Sauté onion in butter until transparent. Add the meat and stir. Add in the crumbled bread, lemon juice and peel, curry powder, almonds, and salt and pepper. When well mixed, transfer to a buttered casserole. Beat eggs. Add scalded milk and bay leaf to eggs, and pour mixture over meat. Set casserole in a larger pan with 1 inch of water. Bake in 350° F. oven until custard is firm, or until knife blade comes out clean. This takes about 30 minutes.

Serve with steamed rice, and chutneys on the side.

SERVES 6 TO 8

ℵ Stendahl's Curry

The first time I heard about curry was long ago in Los Angeles. A family there served Indian food in their home. Once I found the place I thrilled to a throbbing, exotic aroma that led me down a long walk to the little house. I was dismayed to find the family busily polishing tableware and packing up everything to return to India. I left, definitely hooked on just the fragrance of curry.

Later, I tasted my first curry and swooned. What I had, though, was not an Indian curry but one from Fiji, where many policemen, shopkeepers, and restaurant owners are Hindu.

I still prefer this Fijian curry above all others, even after several visits to the Indian subcontinent. In India and America curry means many small dishes, one with meat, one with vegetables, one with relish, and so on. The curry I love most is more like an Indonesian or Chinese dish, all good things piled together on a plate to create a one-dish masterpiece. Try my way and it could make your reputation as a snappy cook.

This version is a very loose but superb dish. The chief admonition is that you must fry the curry, onions, and meat first. Squirt the curry with lime to help tame its raw taste. Next add almost any combination of fresh, crunchy, and colorful vegetables you wish. Finally, adjust the melange so as to achieve a fine meat and vegetable mixture, aswim in a thick gravy. Serve over steamed rice, and accompany with Mango Chutney (following recipe).

> 2 cups cubed cooked meat of any kind (lamb or chicken
>   is fine; I prefer turkey—a strongly flavored meat that
>   takes well to sauces)
> 2 tablespoons butter
> 4 onions, chopped
> 2 cloves garlic, chopped
> 1 heaping tablespoon curry powder (p. 13)
> 5 stalks celery, chopped
> juice of 1 lime
> 4 tomatoes, chopped, or 35-ounce can tomatoes,
>   drained and chopped
> ½ pound fresh green beans, French-cut, or 10-ounce
>   package frozen
> 6 fresh water chestnuts, chopped coarsely, or 1 small
>   can water chestnuts, chopped coarsely
> ½ pound fresh mushrooms, chopped
> any leftovers that appeal to you, coarsely chopped
> ½ cup milk
> 1 cup chicken or beef stock or water, if needed
> 1 tablespoon flour, if needed

Warm meat in butter. Add onions and garlic, stirring well. When onions turn golden, sprinkle in curry powder. Stir. Add celery and lime juice. Stir. Add tomatoes, green beans, water chestnuts, mushrooms, and anything else you like. Stir.

When dish is well simmered, add milk and taste. If thick, add 1 cup stock. If thin, add in the flour, stirring well. (With any luck, the flour will not be necessary.)

SERVES 6 TO 8

🎺 Mango Chutney

Few things go so well with curries as a good mango chutney, with its sweet, exotic flavor. Major Grey's is only one type of fairly sweet chutney. No one seems to know who the Major was, but I agree he had good taste. This mango chutney comes from Hawaii, and if you want to try making your own, I feel sure you'll like it.

    2 pounds fresh mangoes
    1 tablespoon salt
    1 pound sugar
    1¼ cups white vinegar (rice vinegar suggested)
    ¼ pound slivered blanched almonds
    ¼ pound candied orange peel, thinly sliced
    ¼ pound candied lemon peel, thinly sliced
    ¼ pound candied citron, thinly sliced (optional)
    ¼ pound sultana raisins
    3 pieces fresh ginger root the size of a quarter, thinly sliced
    ¼ cup preserved ginger
    1 clove garlic, minced
    3 dried red peppers, seeded and finely chopped
    1 onion, minced

Peel mangoes, slice them into small pieces, add salt, and let sit overnight. The next day, boil the sugar and vinegar together for 5 minutes. Lower heat to simmer. Drain the mangoes of any liquid and add them to the vinegar-sugar mixture. Cook until tender, about 15 minutes. Add the rest of the ingredients and simmer for 30 to 60 minutes, until mixture is thick. Pour into sterilized jars and seal immediately.

MAKES ABOUT 1 QUART

🎵 Vindaloo Curry

Curries from different parts of India have different names. At the mild end of the spicy scale there are *kormas*, which are made with yogurt, cream, or both. At the hot end are the *danshak*, wig-lifters that are not for neophytes. A *keema* curry means the base is ground meat. *Madras* generally means tomatoes, and it's hot. *Pilaw*, or *pilau*, is a pilaf. *Biryani* is a noncurried dish with a pilaf base. *Tandoori* is chicken roasted in a tandoor oven. Because it is covered with red-colored spices, tandoori looks hot, but isn't. It is one of the mildest of Indian dishes. Of all the curries, a *vindaloo* is the hottest. This one comes from Bombay. Note that the spices in this recipe are powdered (or ground), and not left whole as is usual in India.

Note. Ghee is the Indian clarified butter. Traditionally it is prepared from buffalo milk. If you don't have a buffalo handy, melt ½ pound unsalted butter over very low heat. As a bubbly froth rises to the surface, skim and discard. Cool the mixture and carefully pour off the clear yellow oil into a measuring cup. This is ghee, or clarified butter. (Discard the white residue at the bottom of the pan.)

Vindaloo is served with rice and an accompanying bowl of yogurt.

> 1 teaspoon dried red pepper flakes
> ¼ teaspoon mustard seed
> ½ teaspoon powdered ginger
> ¼ teaspoon powdered turmeric
> 2 tomatoes, chopped
> 2 onions, finely chopped
> 1 clove garlic, minced
> 1 tablespoon vinegar
> 10 tablespoons ghee or clarified butter
> 1 pound potatoes, peeled and cubed
> 2 pounds diced cooked meat or fish (chicken, lamb,
>   pork, or shrimp)

In a mortar, grind the pepper flakes and mustard seed well. Add ginger and turmeric, mix well. Place in a mixing bowl and stir in tomatoes, onions, garlic, and vinegar. Heat ghee or clarified butter over a medium flame in a large skillet. Add spice mixture and simmer for 3 minutes. Add the cubed potatoes. When potatoes are nearly cooked (about 20 minutes), add the cooked meat or fish and stir. Stir until meat is heated through.

SERVES 6

Beans, Rice, Pasta, Cheese, & Eggs

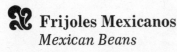 Quick-Soak Method for Beans

My instinct is to hold with tradition and avoid shortcuts. However, this quick-soak method has the support of many knowledgeable cooks—and it certainly saves time.

    1½ quarts boiling water
    1 pound dried beans, washed and picked over
    1 teaspoon salt

Add beans to boiling water. Return to full boil as quickly as possible. Boil *exactly* 2 minutes. Remove from heat, cover, and let stand for 1 hour. Proceed with recipe, using the bean liquid for stock if required.

Frijoles Mexicanos
Mexican Beans

This is an authentic recipe for a Mexican staple, with just enough spice to make it interesting. The beans cannot be kidney beans, but must be the frijole, a red bean with a white stitch in the side. Pinto beans are an acceptable substitute, but none other.

1 pound red frijoles or pinto beans
1 tablespoon lard or vegetable oil
½ teaspoon salt
1 onion, finely chopped
1 teaspoon oregano
1 teaspoon powdered cumin

Pick over the beans; rinse, and soak them overnight in water to cover or use quick-soak method (p. 165). Put the soaked beans and 2 quarts of water in a heavy soup pot. Add lard or oil, bring the beans to a boil, and simmer for 3 hours (add more water as needed to keep beans covered). Add remaining ingredients and cook at least 1 more hour. Test the beans with a fork from time to time for tenderness. During final stages of cooking, mash a few beans against the side of the pot to thicken the liquid. The beans, when ready, should be soupy rather than dry.

SERVES 4

ℵ Frijoles Refritos
Refried Beans

Mexicans always make a bigger pot of beans than they expect to eat at one meal. This entitles them to enjoy a wonderful dish, frijoles refritos, the next day, or even later in the same day. Although essentially the same dish as Frijoles Mexicanos (preceding recipe), the subtle variation makes this a unique gustatory treat unto itself. Not for weight watchers, it's divine nevertheless.

1 tablespoon lard or vegetable oil
3 cloves garlic
1 small onion, chopped
leftover frijoles, at least 2 cups
½ cup sharp cheddar cheese, grated
splash of milk or water, if needed

Heat lard or oil in a heavy skillet over a high flame until blistering hot. Toss in garlic cloves and when they turn brown, discard them. To the oil add the onion, and top it at once with enough beans to fill the pan. Mash the beans with a spatula. Top with grated cheese. Cook slowly. When beans are crusty on the bottom, flip over to crust the other side. If beans seem too dry, add a few drops of milk or water. Beans should form a crusty cake, browned on the outside, meltingly creamy within.

NEVER ENOUGH TO SERVE
EVERYONE PROPERLY

Black Beans, Guatemaltecan

This popular Latin American dish should be known by more North Americans. It is utterly delicious.

    1 pound dried black beans
    1 onion, chopped
    2 cloves garlic, chopped
    3 stalks celery, chopped
    1 fresh hot red pepper, seeded and minced
    1 carrot, finely chopped
    1 herb bouquet (generous pinches fresh parsley and
        thyme, and 1 bay leaf)
    3 tablespoons lard
    generous sprinkling salt
    1 cup or more dry white wine
    2 ounces dark rum
    1 pint sour cream

Wash and pick over beans, and soak them overnight in water to cover or use quick-soak method (p. 165). Drain beans, and toss them in a large ovenproof pot with the onion, garlic, celery, hot pepper, and carrot. Place herbs in a cheesecloth bag and add to beans. Cover with water, bring to a boil, lower heat, and simmer for 3 or 4 hours, until beans are becoming tender. Heat oven to 325° F. Remove herb bouquet. Add lard and salt to beans and stir. Add wine until combined liquids cover beans. Cover and bake until tender, 1 hour or more. Just before serving, sprinkle with the rum.

Decorate each serving with a large dollop of sour cream.

SERVES 4

🎕 Oriental Steamed Rice

Long ago, when I was very young, I was taught the Oriental way to make perfect rice, literally at the hands of that beauteous seductress of the silent screen, Anna May Wong. What she told me proved to be utterly true: You must use a heavy pot with a tight-fitting lid, and—no matter how much rice you're making—you must cover it with water to the depth of one knuckle. On the slender finger with which the lovely Anna demonstrated, a knuckle probably equaled ¾ of an inch. If you follow this foolproof method, your rice will never fail. Below are proportions to give you a generous amount of rice, suggested in a number of recipes in this book.

>   2 cups rice
>   3 cups water, approximately
>   1 teaspoon peanut oil

Unless the package states otherwise, "wash the rice in seven waters" until the water runs clear; the washing gets rid of any protective talc the rice might have.

In a heavy pot with a tight lid, put in the rice, cover with water to the depth of one knuckle, add the teaspoon of oil. Bring rice to boil. When little "wells" begin to appear in the rice, set lid on firmly, turn heat very low (or set pot on a slow-heating pad), and steam for 15 minutes. *Do not peek!*

Remove pot from stove and, using chopsticks or a fork, but never a spoon, gently fluff the rice from the bottom. Put lid back on and let sit for 5 minutes. In a good pot, rice will stay warm at least 30 minutes.

Rice made this way reheats well. Add 1 tablespoon cold water to each cup of cooked rice and steam, tightly covered, for 8 minutes. The steam will fluff the rice perfectly.

MAKES 6 CUPS, ENOUGH FOR 4 TO 6

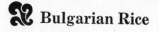 Bulgarian Rice

Here is rice with a good bite to it. Try it with veal, chicken, or lamb chops.

    2 tablespoons lard or vegetable oil
    2 cups long-grain rice
    1 medium onion, chopped
    2 dried red peppers, seeded and minced
    1 clove garlic, minced
    4 cups water or stock
    ½ teaspoon salt

In a heavy pot with tight-fitting lid, heat the lard or oil. Sauté rice, onion, peppers, and garlic over medium heat, stirring occasionally, until rice is golden brown. Add water or stock and salt. Turn up heat and bring to a boil. Cover and simmer for 15 minutes, until rice is fluffy and dry.

SERVES 6 TO 8

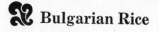 Pilaf

Also spelled *pilau*, this is distinctly a cousin to the Italian risotto and the Spanish base for paella and arroz con pollo. It goes beautifully with Middle Eastern or Indonesian feasts. It also makes a splendid accompaniment for a baked ham.

½ pound (2 sticks) plus 1 teaspoon butter
1 large onion, finely chopped
1 clove garlic, minced
2 cups long-grain rice
pinch powdered cloves
pinch powdered cinnamon
pinch powdered allspice
dash Tabasco or cayenne
1 teaspoon salt
boiling water, as needed
¼ cup sultana raisins
2 tablespoons slivered blanched almonds

In a heavy pot with a lid, melt ½ pound of butter, and sauté onion and garlic until golden. Add the rice and stir steadily for about 5 minutes, until golden and translucent. Add the spices and salt, then pour enough boiling water onto rice to cover it by about ½ inch. Cover the pot tightly and simmer on lowest heat for 20 minutes. Don't peek! When it is cooked, fluff the rice lightly, lifting from the bottom with a fork (not a spoon!). In a small skillet, melt remaining teaspoon of butter, and toss the raisins and almonds until the nuts begin to brown. Sprinkle over the rice, and serve.

SERVES 6 TO 8

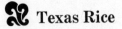 Texas Rice

This is a beautiful side dish for almost any Latin specialty. It goes particularly well with a casserole, and like pilaf it complements an American baked ham perfectly. Using beer as the liquid for the dish adds a subtle yeasty flavor.

2½ tablespoons olive oil
4 cloves garlic, mashed
2 onions, finely chopped
pinch saffron
pinch dried red pepper flakes
1 cup long-grain rice
1 whole pimiento, chopped
1 ripe tomato, finely chopped, or 2 tablespoons
    tomato purée
1½ cups chicken broth or beer

In a heavy pot with a tight-fitting lid, heat the oil and brown the garlic. Remove garlic. Add onions and cook until translucent. Add the saffron and pepper flakes. Add the rice, stirring steadily about 5 minutes, until it becomes golden. Add the pimiento. Sauté gently for 3 minutes. Stir in the tomato. Add the broth or beer and a bit of water, if needed, to cover rice well. When rice boils, cover tightly, turn to lowest heat or put on asbestos pad, and simmer for 15 minutes without peeking. Fluff rice with a fork before serving.

SERVES 4

🙚 Salad Andalusia

This savory main course makes an interesting hot-weather change from the usual tuna or chicken salad. Garlic bread and a good Spanish wine complete the meal.

2 cups cooked rice
2 tomatoes, peeled and cut in thin wedges
2 fresh hot red peppers, seeded and julienned
⅓ cup fine olive oil
1 onion, minced
2 cloves garlic, mashed
2 tablespoons red wine vinegar
1 chorizo (Spanish sausage)

Combine all ingredients except the chorizo, and mix well. Chill thoroughly. To serve, place a mound of salad in center of each plate, and circle with rounds of thinly sliced chorizo.

SERVES 4

🎵 Kid Ory's Red Beans and Rice

Red beans and rice is so intrinsic a Delta dish that Louis Armstrong used to sign his letters "red beans and ricely yours." His colleague in the immortal Hot Five Jazz Band was Kid Ory, a master of Creole cooking as well as of the trombone. This splendid version was given to me by the Kid.

    1 pound red beans, cooked
    1 large onion, chopped
    1½ pounds *hot* smoked sausage
    1 ham hock
    1 bell pepper, seeded and chopped
    2 cloves garlic, minced
    ½ teaspoon dried red pepper flakes
    ½ teaspoon salt
    freshly ground black pepper to taste
    3 cups cooked long-grain rice
    1 handful fresh parsley, finely chopped

Start by preparing beans, which may be done in advance. Wash and clean beans, and soak overnight or use quick-soak method (p. 165). Drain, add fresh water to cover generously. Put in chopped onion, and simmer until tender (3 or 4 hours), adding more water if needed.

When ready to make the dish, simmer the sausage in hot water to cover for 15 minutes. Pour off water and fat. Add the sausage, ham hock, pepper, garlic, pepper flakes, salt, and pepper to beans. Simmer 2 or 3 hours, adding more water if needed to keep mixture moist. When meat is tender and beans impregnated with flavor, remove and slice meat off ham hock and slice the sausages. Mash some of the beans with a wooden spoon to thicken the mixture. Stir meat back in.

During the last 30 minutes of cooking the beans, steam the rice.

When ready to serve, put a scoop of rice in a soup plate, and top with bean-meat mixture. Garnish each plate with parsley.

SERVES ABOUT 6

🎵 Moors and Christians

This tasty combination of beans and rice is a staple for Cubans, who may or may not reflect on the historical significance of its name.

When serving you may enliven the rice by a squirt of fresh lemon juice. A sophisticated touch is to stir 2 tablespoons of mango chutney into the bean pot just before serving.

    1 pound black beans
    4 slices bacon, fried crisp
    1 clove garlic, minced
    1 onion, diced
    1 teaspoon chili powder
    ¼ teaspoon cayenne
    ¼ teaspoon salt
    1 quart meat stock
    2 cups long-grain rice, steamed (p. 168)

Wash and pick over beans, and soak them overnight in a large pot with water to cover or use the quick-soak method (p. 165). Drain beans and return to pot. Add 1½ quarts cold water and bring to a boil. Crumble the bacon into the beans. Add garlic, onion, chili powder, cayenne, and salt. Add stock, lower heat, and simmer about 4 hours, until beans begin to fall apart a little. Sauce should now be rich and thick.

Serve beans over a mound of rice.

SERVES 4

California Enchiladas

I obtained this treasured recipe from a friend who was a waitress in a small-time Los Angeles "Mexican joint." I begged her for it after I left California and realized how much I had begun to miss this great dish. She generously obliged.

Frijoles Mexicanos, Mexican Rice (see recipes), and chilled Mexican beer should always accompany this dish. Serve additional hot steamed tortillas on the side if you wish.

Enchilada sauce
2 tablespoons lard or vegetable oil
2 cloves garlic, mashed
1 onion, finely sliced
5 tablespoons chili powder
½ teaspoon oregano
¼ teaspoon powdered cumin
1 tablespoon flour
1-ounce square unsweetened baking chocolate
1 teaspoon salt
1 quart water, or 2 cups water and 2 cups tomato juice

Melt lard or oil in a pan and lightly brown the garlic and onion. Stir in chili powder, oregano, cumin, flour, chocolate, and salt. When chocolate melts, add the liquid. Simmer for 15 minutes, stirring occasionally, then set over very low heat.

Enchiladas
2 tablespoons lard or vegetable oil
12 corn tortillas
¼ pound Monterey Jack or cheddar cheese, grated
1 pint sour cream
1 onion, finely chopped
3 whole scallions, cut in ¼-inch lengths

In a small skillet, just larger than the tortillas, heat lard or oil. With tongs, dip each tortilla into hot fat for about 30 seconds, then turn to soften on the other side. Place on paper towels to drain. Repeat as quickly as possible until all tortillas are softened. Quickly put a heaping tablespoon of grated cheese on each tortilla, followed by a heaping tablespoon of sour cream, and roll up into a fat crêpe shape to form an enchilada. Save remaining cheese for topping. Line a pan with the stuffed tortillas, leaving a space between each one. Pour the sauce over. Sprinkle with chopped onion, and cover with remaining grated cheese.

The authentic method of cooking is to put enchiladas under a high-flame broiler for about 5 minutes. Or you can bake in preheated 350° F. oven for about 20 minutes, until cheese becomes molten. Just before serving, color the red and yellow crust with bright green scallions. Serve on blistering hot plates.

To steam tortillas: Wrap the tortillas loosely in a dampened napkin, wrap napkin in foil and seal, and warm in a 250° F. oven for 20 minutes. At the table, keep securely wrapped between servings.

SERVES 4 TO 6

🎗 Sour-Cream Enchiladas

This is a New Mexican gringo version of what in Mexico becomes *Enchiladas Suizas*. In the finest style, *Enchiladas Suizas* come dressed in white (sour cream), red (red chili sauce), and green (green chili sauce)—a luscious version of the Mexican flag. This variation is simple to make and divine to taste. If you use canned chilies, the overall flavor is mild indeed, barely qualifying as tangy. Try to use fresh green Anaheim chilies (or green frying peppers), if you can, to lend the dish more character. A crisp green salad, Mexican Rice (see recipe), and iced Mexican beer turn this dish into a rare feast.

The sauce makes a most unusual and delicious dip for crisply fried corn tortilla chips at cocktail time.

3 tablespoons vegetable oil
6 fresh green chilies or 4 cans whole green chilies,
    chopped
12 whole scallions, chopped
5 fresh tomatoes, finely chopped, or 35-ounce can
    tomatoes, drained
1 heaping teaspoon powdered cumin
dash sugar
½ teaspoon salt
freshly ground black pepper
2 cups sour cream
12 fresh or frozen corn tortillas
½ pound Monterey Jack or cheddar cheese, grated

Heat 1 tablespoon oil in a large skillet. Sauté the chilies and
scallions until scallions are limp. Add the tomatoes, cumin, sugar,
salt, and a generous grinding of pepper. Simmer for 15 minutes.
Add the sour cream and stir to make a thick rosy sauce.

In a small skillet, heat 1 tablespoon oil, and soften each
tortilla by dipping in the hot oil for 30 seconds on each side.
Use tongs to turn. Drain tortillas on paper towels.

Fill each tortilla with sauce and roll up to form an enchilada. Lay the enchiladas in a pan with space between each. An
electric skillet is an ideal utensil for this, or heat oven to 350° F.

When enchiladas are filled and stacked, cover with any remaining sauce, and sprinkle tops with the grated cheese.

Cover skillet and simmer for 15 to 20 minutes, or heat in
oven for about 20 minutes, until cheese has melted.

SERVES 4 TO 6

🎵 Noodles in Oyster Sauce, Peking Style

This dish is only delicately tangy, but it is an example of the true Peking style of cooking. Oyster sauce is available in Chinese grocery stores, or see Mail-Order Sources.

½ pound narrow flat Chinese egg noodles
¼ cup peanut oil
1 walnut-size piece fresh ginger, slivered or grated
3 whole scallions, sliced in 1-inch pieces
½ cup chicken stock
oyster sauce

Cook noodles in boiling water until barely done, no more than 3 minutes. Drain. Heat the oil to high heat in a wok or deep iron skillet. Add the ginger and scallions and stir-fry briskly for 2 minutes. Keeping the heat high, add a very little of the stock and cook until liquid disappears. Keep adding more stock a bit at a time and cook until liquid disappears, stirring constantly. When the last of the stock is almost gone, quickly add the noodles and toss until smoking hot. (They will be a bit shiny from the oil left in the pan.)

Serve with small individual dip dishes of oyster sauce.

SIDE DISH FOR 4

🎵 Pasta con le Sarde
Pasta with Sardines

Everywhere in the bustling capital city of Palermo, Sicily, the hungry traveler will find pasta con le sarde as exotic a combination of fish and pasta as can be found anywhere. This Mediterranean beauty is seldom served outside Palermo, even in Sicily, and it is almost unknown in the United States. Now you have the secret.

Different pasta shapes make for a different dish. Bucatini and perciatelli are macaroni types—the very smallest of the tubes. They are chewier and meatier than spaghetti or linguini, and my special favorites. You may use whatever shapes you can find at your grocer's, but, for the following pasta recipes, *never* use any but imported pasta!

> ¼ cup plus 1 tablespoon finest-quality olive oil (light
>   Sicilian if obtainable)
> 1 cup fresh bread crumbs
> 1 onion, minced
> 2 tablespoons pignolas (pine nuts)
> 1 pound fennel stalks, finely chopped (about 2 cups)
> 8-ounce can tomato purée
> 2 tablespoons currants or raisins
> ¼ teaspoon salt
> freshly ground black pepper
> ½ pound fresh sardines or smelt fillets, cut into 1-inch
>   pieces
> 1 pound perciatelli or bucatini
> 4 salted sardines, rinsed and cut into 1-inch pieces,
>   or substitute Danish sardines

In a small skillet, heat 1 tablespoon olive oil over medium flame, and toss bread crumbs until they are toasted a golden brown. Drain on absorbent paper.

Heat ¼ cup olive oil in a heavy skillet, and sauté the onion, pignolas, and fennel for about 3 minutes, stirring constantly. Add the tomato purée, currants or raisins, salt, and a generous grinding of pepper, and simmer for 10 minutes. Add the fresh fish and simmer 10 minutes more.

Meanwhile, cook the pasta until just barely done, drain, and place in a large pre-warmed serving bowl. Add half the sauce to the pasta and mix. Serve the pasta in individual soup bowls, and top each serving with salted sardine pieces and bread crumbs. Pass the rest of the sauce in a serving bowl, for each guest to help himself.

SERVES 4

🦂 Spaghetti alla Bolognese

What Lyons is to France, Bologna is to Italy. One of the greatest of pasta sauces originated there, although many a second-rate sauce has tried to acquire a little class by tacking *Bolognese* to its thin tomato taste. As with all multi-ingredient dishes, no two experts quite agree on what a true Bolognese is. This is *my* classic version—while it may have been matched, it has never been surpassed. *Do not vary the recipe.*

    ½ cup finest-quality olive oil
    2 large onions, finely chopped
    2 cloves garlic, finely chopped
    1 pound lean ground meat (¾ beef plus ¼ pork is best)
    6-ounce can tomato paste
    35-ounce can imported pear tomatoes
    1 tomato can dry white wine or vermouth and same
        of water
    1 teaspoon salt
    freshly ground black pepper
    3 bay leaves
    dash dried red pepper flakes
    ½ teaspoon oregano
    ¼ teaspoon basil
    ¼ teaspoon sage
    ¼ teaspoon thyme
    ¼ pound fresh mushrooms, chopped
    4 ounces pasta per person
    ¼ pound Parmesan cheese, grated

Heat the olive oil in a deep iron pot. Add the onions, stir until translucent, then add garlic and stir until it takes on color. Add the ground meat and stir until it loses redness.

Add tomato paste. Add tomatoes, breaking them up with a wooden spoon. Fill tomato can with dry white wine and add to pot. Fill again with water and add to pot. Stir to mix and lower heat to simmer. Add the salt, a generous grinding of pepper, the bay leaves, pepper flakes, oregano, basil, sage, and thyme. Simmer for 30 minutes, stirring occasionally to prevent scorching.

Now add the chopped mushrooms and mix in. Simmer for at least 1 hour longer—but the sauce will not reach its perfect stage until after 3, 4, or even 5 hours of very low simmering, with occasional stirring. Adjust seasoning.

Spaghetti or linguini are the proper pastas with this sauce. Allow 4 ounces per person, and test constantly the last few minutes of cooking. The pasta should still be the tiniest bit too firm when pulled out, drained, and slapped into a warm bowl. Pasta continues to cook even after being removed from its liquid; if a tiny bit too firm when yanked from the pot, it will cook to perfection as it is being mixed with the sauce. This is the true secret of real *al dente* pasta.

Fork into soup bowls, top each bowl with a small ladle of rich sauce, and serve. The grated cheese should be in a separate bowl for guests to add as they desire.

MAKES ABOUT 5 CUPS SAUCE, ENOUGH
TO SERVE 8 TO 10 PEOPLE

 ## Pasta alla Norma
Pasta and Eggplant

Vincenzo Bellini was born in Catania, Sicily. His most famous opera was *Norma*. Small wonder that wherever you go in Trinacria you can obtain this most delectable pasta with eggplant, or pasta alla Norma. It has become one of my favorite ways of preparing pasta.

2 small eggplants, sliced crosswise in ½-inch slices
salt
1 pound fresh plum tomatoes, or 35-ounce can tomatoes,
    drained
¼ cup olive oil, plus 3 tablespoons
2 cloves garlic, mashed
½ teaspoon dried red pepper flakes
few sprigs fresh basil
freshly ground black pepper
1 pound spaghetti or other pasta
4 tablespoons grated Romano cheese

Place sliced eggplant in a colander, sprinkle with ½ teaspoon salt, weigh slices down with a heavy plate, and leave them for 30 minutes to drain out their natural "bitterness." Plunge fresh tomatoes into boiling water for 2 minutes to loosen their skins. Remove and peel and seed them. Chop tomatoes coarsely.

Heat ¼ cup olive oil in an iron skillet and add the garlic. When garlic begins to color, add the tomatoes, pepper flakes, and basil, plus ½ teaspoon salt and generous grinding of pepper, and sauté for 15 minutes. Set aside and keep warm. Now blot the eggplant slices dry.

Meanwhile prepare spaghetti or other pasta according to package directions.

While pasta cooks, quickly fry the eggplant slices in a separate skillet in 3 tablespoons hot olive oil, flipping to brown both sides. Remove with spatula to a warm plate.

When pasta is just barely *al dente,* drain and place in a heated serving bowl. Add sauce and toss lightly. Top with the eggplant slices, and toss again to mix well. Serve while very hot. Pass grated Romano for each guest to sprinkle to taste.

SERVES 4

꣚ Pasta all' Amatriciana
Pasta with Pancetta

It is well worth the effort to find a source for pancetta for this sauce. Pancetta is an Italian uncured bacon, sold rolled up jelly-roll style. There is no adequate substitute for its delicate yet definite character. However, you may, if you must, use the best-quality lean bacon obtainable. Spaghetti is the proper pasta for this tasty sauce. Bucatini or perciatelli also suggested.

2 tablespoons butter
3 tablespoons olive oil
1 onion, minced
1 slice pancetta, cut into strips ½ inch wide and 1 inch
    long, or 2 strips good bacon, cut into tiny squares
1 pound fresh plum tomatoes, finely chopped, or
    35-ounce can plum tomatoes, drained and chopped
1 small dried red pepper, seeded and minced, or ½
    teaspoon dried red pepper flakes
salt to taste
1 pound pasta
3 tablespoons freshly grated Parmesan cheese, or 1½
    teaspoons grated Parmesan and 1½ teaspoons grated
    Pecorino

Heat butter and oil in a skillet and sauté onion until it is translucent. Add pancetta or bacon. Sauté for 1 minute more. Add
tomatoes, pepper, and about 1½ teaspoons salt. Cook uncovered
over medium heat for about 25 minutes. Taste for salt. Meanwhile, warm a serving bowl in a 250° F. oven.

Drop pasta into 4 quarts boiling salted water. Cook for 5
to 10 minutes, testing pasta after 5 minutes. When *al dente,*
drain at once. Remove heated bowl from oven and place pasta
in bowl, where it will continue to cook. Add sauce and mix.
Sprinkle cheese over top and serve at once.

SERVES 4

 **Pesto alla Genovese**
Classic Pasta Sauce

Every Genovese housewife will tell you that her recipe for this
most delectable of pasta sauces is better than the one I offer.
However, I have eaten my way through a dozen or so variations
on the theme, and remaining absolutely faithful to the basic
ingredients, I have arrived at what I believe to be the perfect
proportions. It is useless to attempt this sauce without fresh basil.
Spaghetti or linguini are the preferred pastas for this sauce.

1 cup packed fresh basil leaves
4 fat cloves garlic
2 tablespoons chopped fresh flat-leaf parsley
1 teaspoon coarse salt
2 tablespoons pignolas (pine nuts) or walnuts
1 cup grated imported Parmesan cheese
2 tablespoons grated Romano cheese
1 cup fine olive oil
3 tablespoons butter
hot pasta cooking water

Put the basil, garlic, parsley, and salt into a mortar. Grind with a circular motion until you have pestled ingredients to a paste. Add the nuts and use the pestle again. Slowly add the cheeses, pestling all the while, until you arrive at a creamy paste. Add the olive oil slowly, still pestling, until the paste is as rich and creamy as you can get it.

To serve, put 1 heaping tablespoon pesto per person into a small bowl, add a lump of butter, about ½ teaspoon, and a spoonful or less of the hot water from the pasta pot. Be careful not to dilute the creaminess of the sauce with too much water. Add cooked pasta and put another dollop of sauce in its center, letting each guest mix his own at the table. Pass additional cheese for topping as desired.

Pesto can also be made in a blender by putting all ingredients into the blender and mixing until creamy, but the texture is not the same.

If you wish to freeze the pesto, put all ingredients *except* the cheese and butter into the blender. Empty mixture into a jar, top with a little olive oil, and seal tightly.

When you're ready to use, thaw pesto and beat in the grated cheese, the butter, and the hot water just before using. Surplus pesto keeps a long time refrigerated. A spoonful transforms scrambled eggs, sparks a vegetable soup, and adds a new dimension to fresh broccoli.

ABOUT 2 CUPS

 Pizza Dough

This serves as the base for one family-size pizza with the usual tomato and cheese topping; or use it to make Pizza Rustica or Pizza Margherita.

    1 package yeast
    1 cup water
    1 tablespoon lard
    1 tablespoon butter
    1 pound flour
    1 teaspoon salt

Dissolve the yeast in ¼ cup lukewarm water. Put lard and butter in large bowl and pour in ¾ cup rapidly boiling water. When cooled to body temperature, mix in the yeast, flour, and salt. Knead on floured board, adding more flour as needed so the dough doesn't stick to your hands. When dough is smooth and springy, set in buttered bowl in a warm place to rise. When double in bulk, punch down and knead again. Heat oven to 450° F. Roll out dough and stretch it as thinly as possible to cover a pizza pan or baking sheet.

    Add desired topping and bake for about 10 minutes until edges are crisp and toasty.

SERVES 4

 Pizza Rustica

This is a sturdy pizza for those times when the peasant in you has to be satisfied. Definitely not for the bland crowd.

1 recipe pizza dough (preceding recipe)
½ pound thick-sliced bacon, diced
1 teaspoon rosemary, crushed in a mortar
½ teaspoon oregano
½ teaspoon sage
1 tablespoon vegetable oil
½ teaspoon cumin seed
¼ teaspoon dried red pepper flakes

Heat oven to 400° F. Prepare pizza dough, but do not roll out; set aside. Fry the bacon lightly, drain, and put on paper towels. Crumble the rosemary, oregano, and sage with half the cooked bacon. Mix well into the pizza dough. Oil a 10-by-15-inch baking sheet. Roll out the dough as thin as possible, so it entirely fills the sheet. Sprinkle the top with cumin seed, pepper flakes, and the rest of the bacon. Bake for about 25 minutes.

SERVES 4

ℜ Pizza Margherita

There are dozens of pizza styles. The one that has become the all-American favorite is closest to the traditional Italian pie called Margherita.

1 recipe pizza dough (see recipe)
1 pound peeled, seeded, and chopped tomatoes, or 1-pound
    13-ounce can Italian plum tomatoes, drained
1 pound mozzarella cheese, cubed
2 heaping teaspoons oregano
3 tablespoons olive oil

Lightly oil a pizza pan or a 10-by-15-inch baking sheet. Roll out dough to fit, pinching edges to make a slight rim. Paint over thickly with tomatoes. Dot with the cheese, sprinkle with oregano, and dribble on a coating of oil. Bake in a preheated 400° F. oven on lower shelf for about 30 minutes or until edges are crusty. Serve direct from oven.

SERVES 4

🙿 Chiles Rellenos con Queso
Chilies Stuffed with Cheese

A great Mexican dish and one of my special favorites. Do your utmost to get fresh green Anaheim chilies—the canned varieties lack true flavor.

> 6 fresh green chilies, seeded and carefully halved, or
>   2 cans whole green chilies
> about ½ pound Monterey Jack cheese, grated
> 2 eggs, separated
> 1 heaping tablespoon flour
> ¼ teaspoon salt
> 2 cups vegetable oil
> 4 tablespoons taco sauce or other Mexican hot sauce, such
>   as Salsa Borracha (p. 225) or Jalapeño Sauce (p. 228)
> 1 cup shredded lettuce

If the chilies are fresh, spear them with a long fork and blacken the outside over charcoal or gas flame. Wrap in a wet kitchen towel for a minute to steam, and loosen skin. Pull off skin, being careful to keep chilies intact. For canned chilies, carefully unroll them so they can be stuffed. Stuff chilies with the cheese, and gently squeeze to shape them.

Beat the egg whites until stiff. Beat the yolks until lemon-colored. Fold the whites into the yolks and add the flour and salt. Dip chilies in the batter and fry in very hot deep fat until golden, turning once. To serve, garnish with a stripe of one of the sauces. Dress side of dish with shredded lettuce. As with all Mexican food, chilis rellenos must be served piping hot or they will not taste right.

SERVES 3 AS A LUNCHEON DISH,
OR 6 AS A SIDE DISH WITH A
MEXICAN MEAL

 ## Eggs in Clover

These are really eggs in clove–r. They are a refreshing change
from the ordinary egg breakfast dish. I have a trick for using
cloves or any other bouquet garni of herbs in a dish. I stuff them
into a tiny aluminum tea ball, anchor it to the side of the pan,
and yank it out when the dish is ready. No muss, fuss, or cloves
to startle you unexpectedly.

    4 pieces toast
    4 teaspoons butter
    4 strips bacon
    about 1 pint milk
    6 whole cloves
    4 eggs
    4 tablespoons finely chopped fresh parsley

Make crisp toast, butter it lightly, and keep warm. Meanwhile
fry the bacon crisp. Set bacon aside. Pour out most of the bacon
grease and discard. Pour enough milk to just float 4 eggs in the
bacon-greased pan for poaching. Heat but do not boil. Add the
cloves, then the eggs. Spoon milk over eggs to seal tops. As
eggs begin to seal, add parsley.

    Place buttered toast in small deep dishes, 2 slices to each
dish. Add 1 egg to each slice, and sprinkle the crumbled bacon on
the eggs. Remove cloves and pour most of the milk and parsley
over eggs. Serve at once while dish is very hot.

SERVES 2

𝒜 Froscia di Peperoni, Patate, e Uova
Sicilian Peppers, Potatoes, and Eggs

Sicilians adore spicing up everything, from pasta to fish. This
hearty omelet would be good at breakfast or lunch.

¼ cup olive oil
3 large green Italian frying peppers, seeded and cut
   into strips
1 large onion, sliced
2 medium potatoes, boiled, peeled, and sliced
8 large eggs
2 tablespoons water
½ teaspoon salt
freshly ground black pepper to taste

Heat oil in a large skillet, and sauté peppers for 5 minutes. Add
onion and potato slices and sauté 5 minutes more. Beat the eggs
lightly with the water, salt, and pepper, and pour over vegetables. Cook over low heat, pulling eggs to sides of pan with
spatula until they are no longer runny. Invert skillet over large
plate and slip the omelet back to cook the other side for about
2 minutes.

SERVES 4

𝒜 Huevos Rancheros
Poached Eggs Mexican Ranch-Style

This can be a delightful change as a breakfast dish. If you wish
to be authentic, put each egg on a fried tortilla, then top with
sauce.

8 eggs
35-ounce can tomatoes
2 medium onions, finely chopped
1 clove garlic
½ teaspoon dried red pepper flakes
1 teaspoon finely chopped cilantro (fresh coriander)
1 tablespoon red wine vinegar
salt to taste
8 corn tortillas, crisply fried (optional)

Poach eggs until done to taste. Meanwhile combine all remaining ingredients and blend until smooth in blender. Pour into small pan, heat well, and serve at once.

Fry tortillas, one at a time, in a little hot oil for about 1 minute, turning them once. Watch so they don't burn.

SERVES 4

Vegetables

A Word about Cooking Vegetables

Few cooks can beat the Chinese at turning out delicious vegetables. The reason is that they use the merest dab of oil, very high heat, and the briefest cooking time, so that the vegetables are crisp, firm, and *just* cooked. Vitamin content and flavor are both exceptionally high.

In the streets of Kuala Lumpur, Malaysia, where "Chinese" is broadened into "Oriental" cooking, I recall seeing vendors preparing tidbits in vast woks suspended over chimneys of glowing charcoal. I would pay my ten or fifteen cents and watch, fascinated, while the street chef bent down and pumped a giant bellows at the lower air-hole of the chimney. The huge wok would gradually turn red, and finally a brilliant orange. Only then would the chef pour in a dribble of oil, followed by a handful of greens. So great was the heat that the water content of the vegetables nearly made them explode, as they became almost instantly cooked by their internal steam. Seconds later I would be served the freshest, crispest, most flavorful vegetables I have ever tasted. And the color was superb.

A simple American version of wok cookery has become our favorite method of preparing vegetables in our own kitchen. All you will need to follow this technique is a heavy skillet or cast-iron kettle with a tight-fitting lid, some butter, and your vegetables.

Wash the vegetables and cut them into smallish strips or

cubes if necessary. Shake off excess water, but leave them moist. Place a wok or heavy skillet over a high flame for at least 1 minute. Now drop a pat of butter—about 2 tablespoons for four cups of vegetables—into the hot, *HOT* skillet, swish the pan around, and quickly, before the butter turns brown, toss in your vegetables. Slap on the lid and hold it in place while you shake the pan over the flame, tossing the vegetables to coat them with the butter.

After half a minute of shaking, remove the lid and sprinkle with a pinch of salt and any herbs or other seasonings you like, replace the lid, wait a few seconds for heat to build, then turn the heat down to low. Now don't peek! Let the vegetables simmer, tightly covered, for about 3 minutes, and taste. Peas, green beans, and other small and tender vegetables will be ready to serve, piping hot. Asparagus, broccoli, and the like may take 3 or 4 additional minutes of simmering.

Remember, it is the initial very high heat and steam that do the trick. I can't think of any vegetable that can't be made into a dazzling taste treat within minutes by this method, except possibly potatoes (which need longer cooking), and fresh corn on the cob (which demands steaming alone, and that for 2 or 3 minutes, tops).

Try serving vegetables cooked this simple, delicious way. And don't be surprised if your guests stand up and applaud.

🔊 French-Fried Onion Rings—or Eggplant Fingers

It is dismaying that so many restaurants mistakenly serve greasy, dough-coated "balloon tires" and call them onion rings. Onion rings are really simple to make, and there are only two caveats: go as light as possible on the coating, and cook only a few rings at a time. As long as the oil stays very hot, the onion rings should be crisp. Overloading the pot lowers the temperature, and soggy rings are the result. The procedure is exactly the same for deep-fried eggplant.

6 large Bermuda onions (or 1 large eggplant, peeled and
    sliced into finger-size strips)
1 egg, well beaten
½ cup milk
1 cup flour, sifted
dash salt
fat for deep-frying

Peel onions and cut into ¼-inch rings, separating slices, or slice
eggplant into slim fingers. Blend beaten egg and milk. Stir in
flour and salt to make a thin batter. Dip onion rings or eggplant
fingers in batter to coat evenly. In large pot heat 3 inches of fat
to 375° F. Add one small batch of vegetables at a time to the hot
fat until they turn golden. Remove and drain, and keep warm
in oven on a platter covered with paper towels, adding each
batch until complete.

    Note: For Tournedos Caprice (see recipe) or other dish when
only a garnish is needed, scale down batter for one large onion.
Heat fat, about 1½ inches deep, in skillet, and fry 4 rings at a
time.

SERVES 6

🎵 Spicy Fried Onions

A dash of Tabasco or a pinch of cayenne can add flair to almost
any kind of dish—a creamed soup, a sauce, a vegetable. There is
something about a *tiny* bit of Tabasco or cayenne in a mild soup
that, while it does not make it spicy, adds an intriguing under-
note. You should not be aware of the heat, but miss it only if it
were lacking.

    As you gain command of your spices, you'll perform noble
experiments. You might gain confidence by preparing this dish
and the following one. Note that they are not radically altered
from old favorites; they are merely given a push toward a new
dimension. Try these, then invent your own.

4 onions
2 tablespoons oil, butter, lard, or a mixture
⅓ teaspoon thyme or marjoram
good pinch cayenne or generous dash Tabasco
salt and freshly ground black pepper to taste

Peel and thinly slice the onions and separate them into rings. Heat fat in a heavy iron skillet over a high flame. Add the onions and all other ingredients. Stir gently until the onions glisten with oil. Cover and lower heat to simmer for about 12 minutes, until onions are golden but not mushy. Add more salt and pepper as needed. If moisture collects, cook uncovered over higher heat a few moments to evaporate it.

SERVES 4

🦂 Spicy Fried Potatoes

Another version of the preceding recipe for onions.

4 potatoes
2 tablespoons lard, or 1 tablespoon butter and 1 tablespoon
   oil
pinch rosemary, crumbled
good pinch cayenne or generous dash Tabasco
1 clove garlic, speared on a toothpick
salt and freshly ground black pepper

Heat oven to 250° F. Peel potatoes and slice into thin rounds. Pat dry with a paper towel. In a heavy skillet, heat fat to bubbling but not smoking. Add the rosemary, cayenne or Tabasco, and garlic. Fry the potato rounds over medium-high heat, one layer at a time. Do not overlap the rounds. Remove garlic when it becomes very brown. Turn each layer of potatoes once, cooking until golden on both sides. Remove and keep warm on paper towels in low oven. When all layers are done, salt and pepper to taste and serve at once.

SERVES 4

Kim Chi
Korean Spiced Cabbage

No table would be considered set in Korea if the bowl of kim chi were missing. In Hawaii, where there is a large Korean population, you can buy "instant kim chi" in little plastic packages. Here is one you might want to make from scratch. If you begin to mind the smell, the kim chi is about ready.

 2 pounds celery cabbage
 ½ cup salt
 4 cups water
 1 teaspoon finely chopped dried red pepper flakes
 1 tablespoon sugar
 1 small onion, thinly sliced
 1 clove garlic, minced
 ½ teaspoon finely chopped fresh ginger root

Wash the cabbage and cut it into 2-inch pieces. Add the salt and cabbage to the water, and let it soak for 5 hours. Rinse and drain the cabbage thoroughly, add the other ingredients, and mix well. Press the mix into a crockery jar, cover it, and keep it in a cool place for at least 3 days to ripen. Serve at room temperature.

MAKES ABOUT 1 QUART

Chinese Mustard Cabbage

This makes a nice side dish for many Chinese or Japanese meals. It also adds a sharp accent to a cold buffet, all on its own. Call it a cousin to Kim Chi (preceding recipe).

 1 large head mustard cabbage or celery cabbage
     (about 2 pounds)
 2 tablespoons dry mustard
 ½ teaspoon salt
 2 tablespoons soy sauce
 2 teaspoons white or rice vinegar

Wash cabbage and shake dry. Discard any tough outer leaves. Cut remainder into 1-inch-wide crosswise slices. Put in pot, cover with water, and bring to a boil. Boil for 1 minute. Remove from heat and drain.

Mix remaining ingredients, add to the cabbage, and toss well. Cover and refrigerate for at least 1 hour. Serve well chilled.

SERVES 4 TO 6

🦋 Coliflor al Ajo
Iberian Cauliflower

A dish worth making, if only to prove to a "meat and potatoes man" that cauliflower need not be dreary, damp, and depressing. Prepared in the Iberian manner, it can be a zingy, exciting addition to a meal.

 1 head cauliflower
 ½ teaspoon salt
 juice of ½ lemon
 3 tablespoons olive oil
 4 cloves garlic, minced
 ⅛ teaspoon cayenne
 1 teaspoon white wine vinegar

Pick off green leaves from cauliflower head. Cut bottom stem level, so cauliflower will stand. In a pot large enough to hold entire cauliflower, bring about 6 cups water to a boil, along with salt and lemon juice. Add cauliflower and cook until crisply tender (about 15 minutes).

Meanwhile, heat the olive oil in a small skillet. Sauté garlic until golden, add cayenne and vinegar, and stir. Place drained cauliflower in a dish, add garlic mixture, and serve.

SERVES 6

Uminitas
Bolivian Corn Dish

Corn came from the Americas and still stays there to enrich all cuisines. Uminitas undoubtedly began as a simple kind of tamale and graduated to this casserole. Different, but equally worthwhile, and a grace note to any Latin American meal.

2 cups fresh uncooked corn kernels
2 eggs, beaten
1 tablespoon lard or butter
½ teaspoon chili powder
⅛ teaspoon anise seed
1 teaspoon flour
¼ pound cheddar cheese, thinly sliced

With a paring knife, strip kernels from cobs. Combine eggs with corn. Heat lard or butter in heavy iron skillet and add corn mixture, chili powder, anise, and flour. Stir for 1 minute over medium-high heat. Add half the mixture to a buttered casserole. Cover with half the cheese. Add rest of corn mixture. Top with the remaining cheese. Bake at 350° F. for 30 minutes.

SERVES 4 TO 6

Esquites
Mexican Corn

A splendid accompaniment to any Latin meal. A chemical change takes place that makes this considerably tastier than the humble ingredients seem to suggest. Another Mexican miracle.

4 tablespoons butter
1 large onion, chopped
3 cups fresh corn kernels or three 12-ounce cans kernel
    corn, drained
2 dried red peppers, seeded and finely chopped
1 teaspoon salt

Heat 2 tablespoons butter in skillet and add the onion. When onion is golden, add 2 more tablespoons butter, the corn, red peppers, and salt. Stir well. Continue stirring until corn turns brown. Serve piping hot.

SERVES 4 TO 6

🎵 Humas Enolla
South American Creamed Corn

This involves a bit of work, but such a succulent tamale-like delicacy is well worth it.

12 ears fresh corn, grated (save husks)
⅓ cup flour
2 tablespoons minced fresh basil
½ teaspoon salt
freshly ground black pepper to taste
2 tablespoons lard
1 onion, minced
1 bell pepper, minced
2 small fresh green chilies, seeded and minced
½ teaspoon Hungarian paprika
½ teaspoon cayenne
4 tablespoons cream

Heat oven to 325° F. Mix grated corn thoroughly with flour, basil, salt, and pepper. Melt lard in a skillet over medium heat, and sauté onion, bell pepper, and chilies until limp. Stir in corn mixture, and continue to stir over medium heat for 5 minutes, or until bubbly. Stir in the paprika, cayenne, cream.

Line a baking dish with fresh corn husks. Pour in the hot corn mixture, and cover with additional husks. Bake for 30 minutes. Don't eat the husks!

SERVES 6

ℜ Iman, Junior
Turkish Eggplant in Olive Oil

Iman Bayeldi means "fainting priest." There are many versions of this story; my own favorite follows. To get the point of the tale, you must remember that in olden days oil came in jars big enough for the forty thieves to hide in.

An Iman married, and his bride came to him with a dowry of forty jars of the finest olive oil. For her first meal, the bride surprised her husband with a dish of eggplant cooked in olive oil. He was so delighted he asked for the dish three nights in a row. On the fourth night, the bride told him he could not have the dish: she had run out of oil. He fainted.

This is a less rich offshoot of the famous dish that I call Iman, Junior. For the classic Iman Bayeldi ten times this amount of oil would be used. This version can be served hot with rice as a main dish, or cold as an appetizer. When served as an hors d'oeuvre provide sesame crackers for the spread.

- 1 large eggplant, unpeeled, cut into ½-inch cubes
- 2 large onions, diced
- 3 large tomatoes, coarsely chopped
- 1½ cups finely minced cilantro (fresh coriander) or fresh flat-leaf parsley
- ¼ teaspoon salt
- freshly ground black pepper
- generous dash cayenne
- ⅓ cup boiling water
- 2 cloves garlic, minced
- 2 tablespoons fine olive oil

Layer the eggplant, onions, and tomatoes in a skillet, sprinkling each layer with the minced greens, salt, and generous grindings of pepper. Add cayenne and the boiling water, and top with the garlic and oil. (No liquid should be visible.) Cover tightly and simmer until liquid is reduced to a thick gravy, about 30 minutes.

SERVES 4 AS A MAIN DISH,
8 TO 10 AS AN APPETIZER

❧ Shigi Yaki
Eggplant Roasted Japanese-Style

A distinctly different vegetable dish—simplicity turned into perfection.

    1 teaspoon freshly grated ginger
    ¼ cup soy sauce
    1 small eggplant

Grate ginger into soy sauce and let stand. Roast eggplant by piercing with a skewer and turning often over hot coals or gas fire. When eggplant is soft in the center—about 5 to 7 minutes —remove to plate and slit in half, like a baked potato. Dress each half with ginger and soy mixture.

SERVES 2

❧ Indian Eggplant and Rice

Brinjal, or eggplant, is a staple Indian food. It is seldom served in Indian restaurants in America. Once you taste this recipe, you'll join me in wondering why.

    2 cups long-grain rice, steamed (p. 168)
    4 tablespoons vegetable oil
    2 teaspoons powdered coriander
    1 teaspoon powdered cumin
    1 teaspoon chili powder
    1 teaspoon mustard seed, crushed
    ¼ teaspoon turmeric
    freshly ground black pepper
    1 large eggplant, cubed
    juice of 1 lime
    ½ teaspoon salt
    ¼ cup water

Begin by cooking the rice. Keep it covered and warm.

In a heavy pan, heat the oil and drop into it the coriander, cumin, chili powder, mustard seed, turmeric, and pepper. After 2 minutes, add the eggplant cubes and sauté for 5 minutes. Sprinkle on the lime juice and salt. Add the water and simmer until it evaporates and the eggplant is tender (15 or 20 minutes, depending on how soft you like your eggplant).

Gently stir the hot rice into the mixture, using a fork, not a spoon. Serve immediately.

SERVES 4 TO 6

⅋ Spiced Indian Eggplant

This is good as a hot vegetable course at dinner. It can also be served at room temperature, or chilled, as a cocktail dip.

2 eggplants
4 tablespoons butter
2 large onions, finely chopped
3 ripe tomatoes, sliced in thin wedges
¼ cup fresh ginger cut into matchsticks
1 fat fresh hot green pepper, sliced in thin wedges
1 teaspoon paprika
salt to taste
3 tablespoons chopped cilantro (fresh coriander)

The eggplants are best done if you put them on a charcoal grill, turning them over the hot coals until well done. This results in a delicious husky flavor. For apartment dwellers: Skewer the eggplants, and turn them slowly over a high gas flame for 4 or 5 minutes, until the skin chars and they are about to burst. Then cut and scoop out pulp.

Melt butter in a saucepan, and add eggplant pulp. Add onions and cook 10 minutes, stirring often. Add tomatoes, ginger, peppers, paprika, and salt. Simmer 15 minutes, stirring to prevent scorching. Remove from heat. Add the cilantro.

SERVES 4 AS A VEGETABLE,
6 TO 8 AS AN HORS D'OEUVRE

🔊 Eggplant and Yogurt, India-Style

An unusual dish for Western palates, this can be served as a meal
in itself, or as part of a curry dinner. The blistering cayenne is
tempered by the suave yogurt.

        1 large eggplant
        4 tablespoons vegetable oil
        3 large onions, chopped
        2 cloves garlic, mashed
        1 tablespoon freshly grated ginger
        1 teaspoon powdered coriander
        1 teaspoon powdered cumin
        ½ teaspoon turmeric
        ½ teaspoon salt
        ¼ teaspoon cayenne
        ½ teaspoon sugar
        1 cup yogurt

Heat oven to 350° F. Bake eggplant with skin on until tender,
about 20 minutes. Cool and cube. In a large saucepan, heat 2
tablespoons oil and brown the onions. Add garlic, ginger, coriander, cumin, turmeric, salt, and cayenne. Cook for 5 minutes. Add
2 tablespoons oil and then the eggplant. Cook 5 minutes longer.
Just before serving, stir in the sugar and the yogurt.

SERVES 3 OR 4

ℛ Fragrant Szechuan Eggplant

The Chinese know how to treat eggplant. Of all the versions of this spicy favorite I have encountered, I vote this the best. Serve it with steamed rice.

½ pound boneless pork, in thin shreds
6 tablespoons soy sauce
1 tablespoon cornstarch
2 tablespoons sherry
4 tablespoons sugar
¼ cup white or rice vinegar
¼ cup water
6 tablespoons peanut oil
1 tablespoon seeded and minced dried red peppers
1 large eggplant, diced but not peeled
6 quarter-size slices fresh ginger
4 whole scallions, chopped into 1½-inch sections (white
    and green separate)

The pork shreds should be about 2 inches long, ⅛ inch wide, ⅛ inch thick. Marinate pork in a mixture of 2 tablespoons soy sauce, cornstarch, and sherry. Combine in a bowl 4 tablespoons soy sauce, the sugar, vinegar, and water.

In a wok over medium heat, dribble in 2 tablespoons oil. Add the dried peppers and sauté briefly.

Add the eggplant cubes and sauté, flipping them constantly, until done, about 6 minutes.

Add soy-vinegar mixture and turn heat *high* until eggplant is coated, and sauce is reduced, about 5 minutes. Remove eggplant and set aside.

Add 4 tablespoons oil over *high* heat. Add the ginger and the whites of the scallions; stir-fry 30 seconds.

Now add the pork and stir-fry for 2 minutes. Add the eggplant and stir-fry for 2 minutes. Add the green scallions and stir briefly.

SERVES 4 AS A MAJOR DISH IN A
CHINESE MEAL

🎜 Eggplant Fritters Martinique

These are splendid as cocktail snacks, and they also go nicely as a vegetable for a main dish.

    1 large eggplant
    1 egg, beaten
    2 tablespoons milk
    1 cup all-purpose flour
    1 teaspoon baking powder
    ⅛ teaspoon cayenne
    pinch salt and generous grinding black pepper
    oil for deep-frying

Peel and cube eggplant. Cook in boiling, salted water for 10 minutes, until tender. Drain well and mash into a purée. Add the beaten egg and milk. Sift flour, baking powder, cayenne, and salt and pepper. Beat flour mixture into purée gradually until the purée is smooth. Deep-fry the mixture by tablespoonfuls in very hot oil (375° F.) until golden.

MAKES ABOUT 20 FRITTERS

🎜 Ratatouille

Another famous dish that varies with each hand that prepares it. Start with this version and look for others that might better suit your palate.

    2 tablespoons olive oil
    1 large eggplant, cubed
    3 tomatoes, crushed
    3 zucchini, cubed
    2 medium onions, diced
    2 bell peppers, diced
    1 clove garlic, minced
    2 tablespoons chopped fresh parsley

In the olive oil, sauté all ingredients, except parsley, until soft but not brown, about 6 to 9 minutes. Stir in the parsley and serve.

SERVES 6

🎵 Speedy, Low-Calorie Ratatouille

Marjorie Thorson Parsons gave me my first lesson in serious cooking. Here is her recipe for—believe it or not—a weight watcher's ratatouille.

There is an interesting variation of this recipe for busy working cooks: if you have any leftover lamb, chop the meat and mix cooked with the uncooked ratatouille; stir in a tablespoon of curry powder, and slip the dish into a hot oven for about 15 minutes. *Voilà!* By the time you make a salad, dinner is ready.

1 medium eggplant, peeled and cut into 1-inch cubes
2 medium tomatoes, cut into ½-inch cubes
2 onions, chopped
1 cup chopped celery
1 small dried red pepper, seeded and minced
1 bell pepper, chopped
pinch salt
1 tablespoon flour
8-ounce can tomato sauce

Boil eggplant for about 5 minutes in salted water. While this is going on, assemble the rest of the vegetables and heat the oven to 350° F. Put all vegetables into a casserole, and sprinkle with salt. If you like, add any herbs that appeal to you, such as oregano or basil. Sprinkle flour over top. Add the tomato sauce and mix gently. Bake for 45 minutes.

SERVES 4 TO 6

ℵ Salade Caprice

While this recipe is only mildly tangy, it does have a bit of a bite, and it is handsome to present.

    4 leaves Bibb lettuce
    4 large leaves Belgian endive
    1 avocado, quartered
    1 medium Spanish onion, finely chopped
    3 tablespoons lime vinaigrette (p. 245; substitute lime
        juice for vinegar)

On each spread lettuce leaf, place one endive leaf, cut in half lengthwise, and one quarter avocado. Sprinkle generously with chopped onion, and dress lightly with lime vinaigrette.

SERVES 4

ℵ Witloof

This is a crisp, zestful salad popular in Belgium. I like the name!

    3 heads Belgian endive, chilled
    4 tablespoons olive oil
    2 tablespoons white wine vinegar
    salt and freshly ground black pepper
    1 red bell pepper, seeded and thinly sliced

Break endive into separate leaves, and toss gently in a salad bowl with the oil and vinegar, a dash of salt, and a generous grinding of black pepper. Garnish with pepper slices.

SERVES 6

Gado Gado

An Indonesian salad (served cold) or vegetable dish (served hot). It is excellent as a counterpoint to the highly spiced Indonesian cuisine. Any or all of the vegetables listed below may be used. Be sure to dress the dish attractively: separate the cauliflower into flowerets, arrange the potatoes and the hard-boiled eggs in pretty slices along the top of the platter; garnish the edges of the platter with shredded lettuce or spinach leaves, and so on as your imagination directs. Each vegetable should be cooked separately in lightly salted water and combined afterward.

> Frenched green beans
> cauliflower buds
> escarole and/or spinach
> cucumbers
> squash
> potatoes
> hard-boiled eggs
> shredded lettuce

> *Sauce*
> rice vinegar (optional)
> 1 tablespoon vegetable oil
> 1 dried red pepper, seeded and minced, or ¼ teaspoon
>   dried red pepper flakes
> 2 tablespoons chunky peanut butter
> 2 cups milk
> dash salt

Arrange your choice of vegetables and eggs on a serving platter. Dribble a little rice vinegar on top if you like.

Simmer all remaining ingredients together or until thickened and hot. Pour the sauce down the middle of the dish and serve.

SERVES ANY NUMBER

♊ Mexicali Green Beans

Besides being good to eat, this dish provides a colorful addition to the table.

      2 tablespoons olive oil
      2 pounds fresh young green beans, snapped in half
      1 Spanish onion, chopped
      1 clove garlic, minced
      2 medium fresh green chilies, minced
      2 tomatoes, peeled, seeded, and chopped
      1 teaspoon cider vinegar
      salt and freshly ground black pepper to taste

In a heavy pot, heat oil and sauté the beans over high heat, stirring constantly, for about 2 minutes, until beans are brightly colored. Add the onion, garlic, and chilies, and stir-fry for 4 minutes, or until onion is translucent. Add tomatoes, vinegar, salt, and pepper. Mix well, cover, and simmer for about 10 minutes, until beans are still crisp but becoming tender. Serve hot as vegetable, or chill and serve as an appetizer.

SERVES 6 TO 8

♊ Portuguese Green Beans

This flavorful dish goes well with most meats, but has an especial affinity for lamb. The cilantro—fresh coriander—makes all the difference.

      3 tablespoons olive oil
      1 large onion, thinly sliced
      1 clove garlic, mashed
      3 large tomatoes, peeled and chopped
      1 pound fresh green beans, broken in half
      salt and freshly ground black pepper to taste
      ⅓ cup chopped cilantro (fresh coriander)

Heat the olive oil in a heavy skillet. Sauté onion and garlic in oil until onions are limp. Add tomatoes and sauté for 5 minutes more. Add the beans, salt, and pepper, stir, and cover. Simmer until beans are tender, about 15 minutes. Remove from heat, stir in the cilantro, and serve immediately.

SERVES 4

Dhal
Indian Lentil Purée

The spicier the curry dish, the blander the dhal (sometimes). This supportive dish comes in a wide range from whole lentils to a smooth purée. Something in between is perhaps more interesting in texture. Lentils come in several colors; I like the red or green for eye appeal.

½ pound lentils
2 bay leaves
¼ teaspoon turmeric
1½ teaspoons salt
2 tablespoons finely chopped fresh parsley
4 tablespoons butter
1 clove garlic, minced

Wash and clean lentils and soak overnight in water to cover, or use the quick-soak method (p. 165). Drain. Put lentils in a heavy pan with bay leaves and enough water to cover by 2 inches. Bring to boil, and let simmer for 1 to 2 hours, skimming foam as it appears. Meanwhile, prepare all other ingredients, and add them during last 30 minutes of cooking. Add more hot water, bit by bit, as needed while the dish simmers. The final dish should be between a thick soup and a creamy gravy. Dhal can be puréed or served as cooked, preferably after mashing some of the lentils against side of pot with a wooden spoon.

Dhal may be served as is, but is improved by adding the following:

1 tablespoon oil
1 small onion, thinly sliced
few shreds fresh ginger

Heat oil very hot in a skillet; then add onion. Cook over medium heat, stirring, until onion is a dark moist brown, about 10 minutes. Add ginger, stir briefly, and remove from heat. Top each serving of dhal with a teaspoonful of this mixture.

SERVE AS A SIDE DISH FOR 4

ℒ Parsnips in Stout

It's a puzzle why this interesting vegetable is held in such low esteem in our land. Here is a recipe that is a challenge; it may not win you over to parsnips, but it should make you respect them. Serve as a side dish with chicken, pork, or ham.

2 or 3 parsnips (about 1 pound), peeled and cut into
    2-inch chunks
1 cup stout or any good dark beer
1 stick cinnamon
freshly grated nutmeg to taste
3 whole cloves
½ teaspoon salt
freshly ground black pepper to taste

Put all ingredients together in a saucepan and simmer, covered, until parsnips are tender, about 30 minutes. Remove lid and simmer uncovered for about 15 minutes, until the liquids have thickened into a glaze. Remove the cinnamon stick and cloves.

SERVES 4

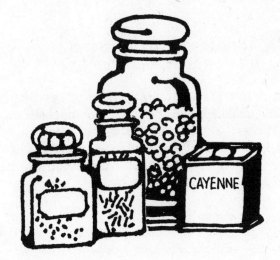

𝕬 Fried Italian Peppers

Here we're dealing with those elegant, slim green beauties in their pristine splendor. Traditional with fried Italian sausage (we prefer the hot variety), but good with any lively foods.

    3 green Italian frying peppers
    2 tablespoons olive oil
    1 large clove garlic, minced
    1 medium onion, thinly sliced and separated into rings
    1 teaspoon cumin seed
    ½ teaspoon oregano
    good pinch cayenne or generous dash Tabasco
    salt and freshly ground black pepper

Halve the peppers lengthwise and remove seeds. Then cut halves into thin strips about ½ inch wide. Heat oil in a skillet, and add pepper strips, skin side down. Sprinkle the minced garlic on top. Add the onion rings, cumin, oregano, cayenne or Tabasco, and salt and pepper to taste. Stir until the mixture glistens with a coating of oil. Cover and simmer for about 5 minutes, or until peppers are tender but not mushy. Adjust salt and pepper and serve hot, as a side dish, or as a covering over meat.

SERVES 3

℘ Rajas Poblanas con Salsa
Green Chilies, Mexicano

This is a Mexican side dish that goes beautifully with morning scrambled eggs, or to grace any Mexican menu. Do not use bell peppers. *Rajas* means slices—in this case, slices of green Anaheim chilies. If you can't get the fresh ones, use the (unfortunately inferior) canned ones or substitute green Italian frying peppers.

> 2 ounces lard or olive oil
> 6 *chiles poblanos* or Anaheim or green frying peppers, seeded
>   and cut into long *rajas*, or strips
> 1 onion, thinly sliced
> juice of 1 fat lemon
> 1 teaspoon salt
> ½ teaspoon freshly ground black pepper
> ½ teaspoon oregano
> ½ teaspoon minced cilantro (fresh coriander) or
>   fresh flat-leaf parsley

Heat lard or oil in skillet; add peppers and onion. Stir until onions are translucent. Add remaining ingredients. Stir just to mix; serve hot.

SERVES 4

℀ Lescó
Hungarian-Style Peppers

This is adapted from a traditional recipe given to me by my friend George Lang, raconteur, designer of innovative restaurants, philosopher of foods, and appreciator of wines, women, and wisdom. It is delicious served cold as an appetizer; served hot, with the addition of meat, it is a tasty main course.

    2 tablespoons olive oil
    1 onion, sliced
    4 green Italian frying peppers, seeded and sliced
        lengthwise
    2 fresh ripe tomatoes, chopped
    1 tablespoon Hungarian paprika
    ½ tablespoon salt
    ¼ tablespoon sugar
    1 tablespoon olive oil (optional)
    ½ pound lean beef (for main dish only)

Heat 2 tablespoons oil and sauté the sliced onion over low heat until translucent. Add pepper slices and cook for about 5 minutes. Add tomatoes, paprika, salt, and sugar, and simmer about 8 minutes.

If the dish is to be served as an appetizer, simply chill it 2 hours or more.

For a main dish: reserve cooked vegetables. Put beef through a coarse grinder (try not to resort to hamburger). Sauté meat in tablespoon hot oil until it loses its redness. Stir in the cooked vegetables. Serve sizzling hot.

SERVES 4

℀ Peperoni Strascinati in Padella
Sicilian Peppers and Eggplants

Sicily, that fabulous museum of mankind, thrives on its plump eggplants and tangy peppers. Note that with a few additions, this dish can be converted into a reasonable facsimile of Caponata alla Siciliana—a sweet-and-sour appetizer of great popularity on the triangle island (following recipe).

> ¼ cup olive oil, or more as needed
> 6 large green Italian frying peppers, seeded and cut
>   into 1-inch slices lengthwise
> 1 large onion, chopped
> 3 celery hearts, coarsely chopped
> 1 plump eggplant, cut in 1-inch cubes
> salt and freshly ground black pepper

In a large skillet, heat the oil and sauté peppers, onion, and celery for 5 minutes. Add eggplant, and more oil, if eggplant begins to stick. Sauté until soft, about 15 minutes. Sprinkle with salt and a generous grinding of black pepper.

This dish may be served hot as a vegetable, or at room temperature, in the Italian style, as an hors d'oeuvre.

SERVES 4

ℜ Caponata alla Siciliana

If you add to the preceding recipe these ingredients, you will have the famous Sicilian appetizer.

> ½ cup pitted green and black olives
> ¼ cup capers
> ¼ teaspoon dried red pepper flakes, or 1 dried red
>   pepper, seeded and minced
> 4 anchovy fillets, chopped
> 1 teaspoon sugar
> ½ cup wine vinegar
> ½ cup water

When the eggplant and peppers are cooked, add the above ingredients. Simmer over low heat until sauce thickens, about 30 minutes.

SERVES 6 TO 8

ꙮ Mofongo
West Indies Plantains

The plantain is larger, less sweet, and starchier than our more familiar banana. This side dish, one of the best of the many Caribbean recipes for plantains, makes an unusual accompaniment for fish, or for fried eggs at breakfast.

> 2 cups water
> ¼ teaspoon salt
> 3 green plantains, peeled and chopped
> ¼ pound salt pork, cubed
> 1 clove garlic, finely minced
> 1 teaspoon powdered cumin

Bring water and salt to a boil, add plantains, and cook for 15 minutes. Drain, mash, and set aside in a large bowl. In a small skillet, fry salt pork until cubes are crisp. Remove pork with a slotted spoon, leaving fat in skillet, and add pork to the mashed plantains. Add garlic and cumin, and blend thoroughly.

Reheat salt pork fat, and press plantain mixture into the skillet to form a solid cake. Brown on both sides, and serve immediately.

SERVES 4

ꙮ Fried Plantains (or Bananas)

In the Hindu religion, the banana, not the apple, was the Forbidden Fruit, a proof of the banana's importance. Here are two tempting recipes for the Caribbean plantain, the banana's first cousin. Served as a vegetable, plantain goes especially well with chicken, pork, or ham.

> *To accompany a meal*
> 6 plantains or firm bananas
> 1 tablespoon butter, oil, or lard
> cayenne (optional)

Peel and halve plantains or bananas lengthwise. Heat fat over medium temperature in a large skillet, and sauté, turning to brown all sides. Sprinkle lightly with cayenne, if you wish, and serve immediately.

SERVES 4

As an hors d'oeuvre
6 plantains or firm bananas
¼ cup butter, oil, or lard
bottled hot pepper sauce

Peel plantains or bananas, and cut into ¼-inch slices. Heat fat over medium flame, and cook slices until crisp. Remove with slotted spoon and drain on paper. Serve with a side dish of hot sauce for dipping.

SERVES 10 TO 12

℞ Spicy Sweet Potato Casserole

This is a mildly tangy variation of an old favorite. It goes well with pork dishes, ham, and of course, poultry, especially turkey.

3 pounds sweet potatoes
12 tablespoons light-brown sugar
4 tablespoons butter
½ teaspoon powdered cinnamon
½ teaspoon freshly grated nutmeg
¼ teaspoon salt
1 cup milk

Cook the sweet potatoes in boiling water until tender (about 20 minutes). Cool potatoes, and peel and mash them.

Heat oven to 400° F. Stir into the mashed potatoes 10 tablespoons of the brown sugar, 3 tablespoons of the butter, and the cinnamon, nutmeg, salt, and milk. Grease a casserole dish with remaining tablespoon of butter, add the potato mixture, and top with the remaining 2 tablespoons of brown sugar. Bake for about 30 minutes.

SERVES 6 TO 8

Sauces, Marinades, & Butters

🎀 Béchamel Sauce

For this book, the classic béchamel must have a little tang: Tabasco, for instance. This is a basic white sauce you will find useful for everyday cooking, whenever you need a light cream sauce. Simple though it is, directions must be followed carefully if you want to achieve a beautiful product.

2 tablespoons butter
2 tablespoons flour
1½ cups hot milk
4 drops Tabasco
½ teaspoon salt
freshly grated nutmeg

In a heavy pan, melt butter over low heat; do not brown. Gradually add the flour, stirring constantly. Let mixture bubble gently about 1 minute, watching it to see that flour doesn't brown. Once blended, remove from heat and add the hot milk all at once, stirring briskly with a wire whisk. Return pan to stove and cook over low heat, stirring until sauce thickens. Remove from heat, add Tabasco, salt, and a generous grinding of nutmeg, and blend well.

MAKES 1 CUP

🎝 Coconut Sauce

This is really a gravy useful for all sorts of curries. It is also often used in the Caribbean as a base for simmering hard-boiled eggs with small cuts in them, or meatballs and such.

> ½ onion, minced
> 1 fresh green chili, seeded and minced
> 1 quarter-size slice fresh ginger, finely chopped
> 1 clove garlic, minced
> ¼ teaspoon curry powder (p. 13)
> dash each powdered cinnamon, fennel seed, powdered
>   cloves, and salt
> 1 cup coconut milk (following recipe)
> ½ cup water (if coconut milk is thick)
> juice of 1 lime

Put all ingredients but coconut milk, water, and lime juice in a pot and heat to boiling point. Remove from heat and slowly add coconut milk, water if necessary, and lime juice. Stir constantly for 2 to 3 minutes or the mixture will curdle.

MAKES ABOUT 1 CUP

🎝 Coconut Milk

Coconut milk is often called for in Latin and Southeast Asian dishes. You can buy it canned in many specialty shops or supermarkets, but here is how to make your own.

> 1 coconut
> 1 cup milk

In a preheated 325° F. oven warm coconut for 15 minutes. Use a corkscrew or a screwdriver and puncture little round "eyes." Drain coconut juice (this is not milk) into a container.

Scrape meat from the coconut, put it into a cheesecloth

bag, and set it in a bowl. Scald the milk, and pour it over the coconut. Let sit for 15 minutes, then squeeze the coconut bag well. Milk should be creamy. If you want a thinner milk, add more hot milk and squeeze again.

 ## Sofrito
Basis for Spanish Sauces

In Puerto Rico and other Caribbean islands, no kitchen can be said to be in full operation without *sofrito* at hand. In big cities *sofrito* can be bought in jars, but it is never as good as the home-made variety, which can be prepared easily in your blender. *Sofrito* is like a Caribbean pistou: a dollop adds enrichment to many kinds of soups and stews. (See Caribbean Arroz con Pollo.)

 ¾ cup peanut oil
 1 large bell pepper, seeded and coarsely chopped
 2 fresh green chilies, seeded and coarsely chopped
 3 onions, coarsely chopped
 6 cloves garlic
 8 sprigs cilantro (fresh coriander)
 1 tablespoon chopped fresh oregano, or 1 teaspoon
    dried
 ½ pound lean cooked ham, chopped
 ¼ teaspoon annatto seeds, or any other saffron-coloring
    agent

Pour ¼ cup of the peanut oil into blender. Add the bell pepper, chilies, onions, garlic, cilantro, and oregano. Blend at high speed for 30 seconds. Add the ham and blend again. In a heavy pot, heat ½ cup of peanut oil, sprinkle on the annatto, and add the contents of the blender. Bring to boiling point, then lower heat and simmer for 15 minutes, stirring occasionally. Cool the mixture and pour into jars. Cover and store in refrigerator until needed. Use 2 or more rounded tablespoons of *sofrito* for a recipe that serves four.

MAKES ABOUT 2 CUPS

🎝 Mohlo de Churrasco
Brazilian Barbecue Sauce

Latin Americans expect to find a small dish of hot sauce on the table, ready to brighten whatever dish is served. This one is a favorite in Brazil. It's good brushed on broiled meats or added in a few splashes to a salad dressing.

    3 cups red wine vinegar
    8 small dried red peppers, seeded and finely chopped
    1 small onion, finely chopped
    2 tablespoons finely chopped fresh parsley
    2 cloves garlic, mashed
    1 tablespoon sugar
    1 tablespoon salt
    1 teaspoon basil
    1 teaspoon marjoram
    1 teaspoon crumbled rosemary
    1 teaspoon thyme

Put all ingredients in a glass jar. Cover tightly and shake well. The sauce will keep in the refrigerator for several weeks.

MAKES ABOUT 1 QUART

🎝 Aji-Li-Mojili Sauce

Here is a Caribbean basting sauce, fine for barbecued pork or chicken and anything else cooked on a charcoal grill.

    6 fresh green chilies, seeded
    4 cloves garlic
    6 peppercorns
    ¼ cup wine vinegar
    ¼ cup lime juice (juice of 2 large limes)
    2 teaspoons salt
    ½ cup olive oil

Mash the chilies, garlic, peppercorns, and vinegar in a mortar—
or spin in a blender about 30 seconds. Place the lime juice, salt,
and olive oil in a bowl. Add the chili mixture, and mix thoroughly. Stir again each time before using. The sauce will keep
a long time if tightly capped and refrigerated.

MAKES ABOUT 1 CUP

 ## Salsa Fresca
Mexican Tomato Sauce

One of a hundred variations, this sauce is simple to make, has a
fine fresh taste, and keeps well if refrigerated. Good for dipping,
excellent spooned sparingly over egg dishes, tacos, enchiladas,
or any other Mexican dish. Fresh cilantro makes an interesting
addition, but it may be difficult to find outside of Latin or Chinese
markets.

    3 large tomatoes, peeled and finely chopped
    3 fresh green chilies, finely chopped
    1 small onion, minced
    1 clove garlic, minced
    pinch finely chopped cilantro (fresh coriander) or fresh
       flat-leaf parsley

Combine all ingredients, mix well, and chill. Allow to mellow
overnight before serving.
    Keeps 10 or 15 days if refrigerated.

MAKES ABOUT 3 CUPS

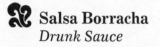

Salsa Borracha
Drunk Sauce

An authentic Mexican hot sauce, useful for spicing tacos or
enchiladas. It's my guess that the reason it's called "drunk sauce"
is because a taste or two would sober up any borracho in a hurry.

4 large tomatoes, peeled and chopped
2 large onions, chopped
4 fresh green chilies, minced
1 cup white wine vinegar
1 teaspoon chopped oregano leaves
½ teaspoon cumin seed, crushed

On the night before you expect the borrachos, mix all ingredients, and blend thoroughly. Store in a covered container. This sauce gains in heat during the night. Pass it in a cup with a spoon so guests can "hot up" their enchiladas or tacos as their palates dictate.

MAKES 2 TO 3 CUPS

Salsa Arabbiata
Enraged Sauce for Pasta

Arabbiata means enraged, hot. So this tomato sauce is a hot one, to be used over pasta or steamed rice. This particular recipe comes from Nicola Zanghi. He and his father, Nino, operate one of the finest restaurants on Long Island. Chef Nicola further suggests that his sauce rabbiata will go well added discreetly to any sautéed foods, such as seafood, pork chops, beefsteaks, or veal. Sauté the meat in light olive oil, add salsa rabbiata, and correct seasonings.

It seems a simple enough sauce, but it transforms pasta into an unforgettable dish.

4 cups peeled and crushed fresh plum tomatoes or
    35-ounce can
½ cup fine olive oil
3 cloves garlic, chopped
1 tablespoon chopped fresh basil leaves
½ teaspoon oregano
½ teaspoon dried red pepper flakes
1 tablespoon salt
1 tablespoon chopped fresh flat-leaf parsley

Simmer tomatoes for 1 hour.

In a large iron pot heat olive oil and sauté garlic over low temperature until translucent. Do not let it burn. Add tomatoes and remaining ingredients. Simmer for 15 minutes.

The sauce will keep for about 1 week in the refrigerator.

MAKES ABOUT 4 CUPS

🎴 Fresh Tomato Sauce

A fresh, light, all-purpose tomato sauce, excellent for pasta—and almost anything else that benefits from a touch of the *pomadoro*.

    1 pound (at least 4 or 5) fresh tomatoes, preferably
       Italian plum-style, peeled
    2 tablespoons butter
    1 tablespoon olive oil
    1 small onion, minced
    1 small bay leaf
    1 teaspoon finely chopped fresh oregano
    salt and freshly ground black pepper
    1 rounded tablespoon chopped fresh basil leaves

Cut cores from tomatoes and chop the pulp. In a skillet, heat 1 tablespoon of the butter with the oil and add onion. As onion turns golden (but before it starts to brown), add the tomatoes, bay leaf, and oregano. Simmer about 15 minutes. Remove bay leaf, pour sauce into blender, purée, and return to skillet. Season to taste with salt and a good grinding of pepper. Reheat and swirl in the remaining tablespoon of butter. Just before serving, stir in the basil leaves.

MAKES ABOUT 2 CUPS

ℜ Jalapeño Sauce for Tacos and Enchiladas

From among countless variations on a theme, here is a melody to make your tacos and enchiladas hum.

    3 cups peeled, seeded, and chopped tomatoes (4 or
        5 large)
    1 clove garlic, minced
    1 small onion, chopped
    1 tablespoon olive oil
    ½ teaspoon oregano
    ½ teaspoon salt
    2 tablespoons canned or fresh jalapeño peppers,
        finely chopped

Mix all ingredients thoroughly. Chill for an hour to meld. Serve cold.

MAKES 1 CUP

ℜ Piquant Sauce from Mexico

A table hot sauce. Dribble it over Mexican dishes at your own discretion. It's excellent for adding tang to a taco.

    2 tomatoes, peeled and mashed
    1 onion, finely chopped
    2 tablespoons wine vinegar
    1 tablespoon corn oil
    1 teaspoon chili powder
    ½ teaspoon dried red pepper flakes
    ½ teaspoon salt

Place all ingredients in a large bowl, and beat until smooth. Transfer to a small serving bowl, and chill. Serve cold.

MAKES 1 CUP

🎜 Barbecue Sauces

Barbecue sauces are innumerable. Here are three nicely sharp examples.

Barbecue Sauce 1

1 large onion, chopped
1 cup catsup
½ cup water
¼ cup lemon juice
¼ cup red wine vinegar
3 tablespoons Worcestershire sauce
2 tablespoons brown sugar
1 tablespoon prepared mustard
½ teaspoon cumin seed
½ teaspoon coarse salt
hearty dash Tabasco
freshly ground black pepper

Combine all ingredients in a large pot, giving a generous grinding of black pepper. Bring to a boil slowly, stirring frequently. Simmer for 30 minutes, stirring occasionally. Will keep indefinitely if refrigerated.

MAKES ABOUT 1½ PINTS

Barbecue Sauce 2 (Rustler's Special)

4 strips bacon, diced
2 onions, finely chopped
2 cloves garlic, mashed
3 cups tomato purée
2 teaspoons soy sauce
1½ teaspoons salt
1 rounded teaspoon chili powder
¼ cup dry mustard
2 teaspoons Hungarian paprika
⅛ teaspoon cayenne
½ cup dark corn syrup or molasses
¼ cup brown sugar
1 bay leaf

Sauté bacon and onions in a big iron pot until onions are translucent and bacon crisp. Add all other ingredients, cover, and simmer for 1 hour. Will keep for weeks if refrigerated.

MAKES ABOUT 1 QUART

Barbecue Sauce 3 (Western Sauce)

1½ cups water
⅓ cup brown sugar
2 cups catsup
⅓ cup vinegar
2 tablespoons cumin seed
½ teaspoon celery seed
freshly ground black pepper
no salt!

Combine all ingredients in a saucepan, generously grinding the pepper. Bring to slow boil and simmer gently for 20 minutes. Use to baste meats while barbecuing. Save at least half to reheat and pour over meat when it is served. Keep surplus sauce in the refrigerator for future use.

MAKES 1 QUART

Sauce Belmont

This is a fine sauce to enliven an everyday meat loaf. It is also delicious streaked over individual small steaks.

3 tablespoons butter
¼ cup catsup
1 tablespoon fresh lemon juice
1 teaspoon Worcestershire sauce
1 teaspoon dry mustard
dash Tabasco
¼ teaspoon freshly grated nutmeg
salt and freshly ground black pepper to taste
2 tablespoons good sherry

In a small saucepan, melt butter and gradually add all other ingredients. Bring to a boil and remove from heat at once.

MAKES ENOUGH SAUCE FOR 1 MEAT LOAF OR 6 STEAKS

🎵 Calypso Chili Sauce

A Caribbean hot sauce that should be served in a separate bowl, to spice up soups or casseroles.

3 pounds tomatoes, peeled and finely chopped
½ pound onions, finely chopped
½ cup brown sugar
1 tablespoon salt
1 cup malt vinegar
1 teaspoon seeded and minced fresh hot red peppers

Bring all ingredients to a boil. Lower the heat and simmer, stirring frequently, until mixture becomes quite thick. Keeps well if refrigerated.

MAKES 3 CUPS

🎵 Catalonian Hot Sauce

From the northern part of Spain comes this spicy sauce. It goes well with meat and game, and the Spaniards like it with shellfish.

½ cup blanched almonds, crushed
4 cloves garlic, mashed
1 tomato, peeled, seeded, and chopped
1 small dried red pepper, seeded and minced
1 cup olive oil
¼ cup red wine vinegar
salt

Preheat oven to 350° F. Place almonds in a pie tin and toast about 10 minutes, until golden. Mix almonds, garlic, tomato, and red pepper together to form a paste. As you mix, very slowly dribble in 2 tablespoons of the oil. Gradually add the vinegar and the rest of the oil, continuing to mix until you achieve a thick sauce. Add salt to taste. Serve at room temperature.

MAKES ABOUT 1½ CUPS

❧ Sorrel Sauce

You can add fresh chopped sorrel to almost any cream sauce, mayonnaise, or hollandaise-type sauce with delectable results. Here is a quick-to-do version for nonspecial occasions that perks up light meats, poultry, or fish. If you are serving the sauce with seafood, use fish stock. Sorrel is also known as sour grass, and is obtainable in season in Jewish or Italian neighborhoods. It is one of my special favorites as a flavoring.

> 2 cups finely chopped fresh sorrel leaves
> 4 teaspoons butter
> 1 teaspoon flour
> 1 cup cream (either light or heavy)
> 2 tablespoons fresh chicken stock (or fish stock for
>   seafood dishes)
> dash freshly grated nutmeg
> salt and freshly ground black pepper to taste

Clean and chop sorrel leaves, discarding coarse stems. Sauté sorrel leaves in 1 teaspoon butter just until wilted. Set aside.

Make a roux: melt the 3 teaspoons of butter over medium heat, add flour, and stir briefly to blend smoothly. Let mixture bubble gently about 1 minute while you heat the cream and stock separately. Add the hot stock to the roux (off heat) and whip briskly with a wire whisk. Quickly add all the hot cream and whisk well. Return to low heat and bring just to boiling point, stirring constantly. Remove from heat. Add the sorrel leaves and the seasonings. Serve very hot or very cold, to suit the main dish.

MAKES 1 CUP

❧ Skordalia
A Greek Sauce

I love this sauce for its garlic, and for the interesting sound of its name. It goes very well with fish and other seafoods, and with cooked greens or potatoes.

4 cloves garlic
1 teaspoon salt
1 slice white bread
¾ cup olive oil
1 egg
juice of 1 lemon
2 tablespoons crushed or chopped pistachio nuts
(optional)

Mash the garlic cloves with the salt. Shred bread into small bits. Put garlic mixture and bread in a blender, and add ¼ cup of the oil and the egg. Blend until smooth, then slowly add ½ cup of olive oil in a thin stream. Add the lemon juice. Blend until smooth. Pistachio nuts may be stirred in after final blending. Serve at room temperature.

MAKES 1 CUP

 Pungent Oriental Marinade

Catsup was invented by the Chinese, but Burgundy was not. This is obviously an American adaptation. Substituting dry sherry for the Burgundy would make it more authentic, but I prefer this marinade in its corrupt form.

½ cup olive oil
¼ cup soy sauce
½ cup Burgundy
2 tablespoons catsup
2 tablespoons minced candied ginger
2 cloves garlic, minced
1 tablespoon curry powder (p. 13)

Mix all ingredients together. Pour over meat or poultry and marinate for 12 to 36 hours in refrigerator.

MAKES 1½ CUPS

✿ Kanazaki's Teriyaki Marinade

All over Japan, each tiny bar has its own special dipping sauces. You sip your drink and dunk deep-fried bits of vegetables or fish as the bartender serves them up, smoking hot. Teriyaki stands also abound, turning out delicately charcoaled chicken tidbits as a snack or, in quantity with rice, as a meal. My good friend from Tokyo, Tsuneo Kanazaki, gave me his own secret version of this recipe, to be used as either a dip sauce or a teriyaki marinade.

> 1 cup top-quality soy sauce
> 2 teaspoons sesame oil
> 2 ounces Mirin sake (Japanese rice wine) or dry
>   vermouth or sherry
> 1 whole scallion, minced
> 1 quarter-size slice ginger, minced
> 1 clove garlic, mashed
> dash dried red pepper flakes
> tiny pinch sugar

Put all ingredients in a bowl and mix well.

This is good as a dipping sauce for tempura or other cocktail tidbits, such as carrot or celery sticks and raw mushrooms.

Or marinate chicken pieces in the mixture for several hours, turning occasionally. As you charcoal-broil the chicken, keep basting with the marinade.

MAKES ABOUT 1½ CUPS

✿ Nuoc Mam Sauce
Vietnamese Dipping Sauce

Nuoc mam sauce is common to Southeast Asia. You can buy the ready-made sauce, imported from the Philippines or Thailand, in any large-city Oriental market. The basic sauce is often called simply "fish sauce," and under that name it can be purchased by mail order. If you cannot obtain fish sauce, you can substitute a good imported soy sauce, and add a generous dab of anchovy paste.

This recipe is an improvement over the simple commercial version.

> 1 cup fish sauce, or 1 cup fine soy sauce plus dab of
>   anchovy paste
> 1 tablespoon minced fresh ginger
> 2 cloves garlic, minced
> 1 teaspoon dried red pepper flakes, or 5 shakes Tabasco
> 3 tablespoons lemon juice
> 2 tablespoons sugar
> ¼ cup water

Mix all ingredients and let stand for a while. Serve in small portions to each guest. Leftover sauce will keep several weeks if refrigerated.

MAKES ABOUT 1 CUP

😵 Piquant Marinade for Chicken or Rabbit

For a succulent, unusual taste, let the meat rest in these juices overnight, and baste during the roasting.

> 1 cup dry white wine
> 1 small onion, thinly sliced
> 4 tablespoons olive oil
> ½ teaspoon rosemary, crushed
> ½ teaspoon juniper berries (about 6), crushed
> freshly ground black pepper
> dash powdered cloves
> pinch cayenne, or dash Tabasco

Mix all ingredients well; use as marinade and basting sauce.

MAKES ABOUT 1½ CUPS

❧ Spicy Dip Sauce for Fish or Meat

If you're having a simple dinner that features fried fish or meat-balls, you can tang them up with this sauce, made in a few minutes. Watch the Tabasco.

    1 cup catsup
    1 tablespoon freshly grated horseradish (or bottled kind)
    1 tablespoon Worcestershire sauce
    dash Tabasco
    dash lemon juice

Mix all ingredients. Serve as a dip sauce.

MAKES 2 CUPS

❧ West Indies Dip Sauce

This typical Creole sauce is good with poultry or fish dishes. If served with fish, use fish stock instead of chicken.

    3 tablespoons vegetable oil
    1 onion, finely chopped
    1 bell pepper, seeded and chopped
    3 tablespoons all-purpose flour
    2 medium tomatoes, chopped
    1 cup chicken stock or dry white wine
    1 teaspoon lime juice
    1 teaspoon wine vinegar
    salt and freshly ground black pepper
    dash (or more) hot pepper sauce

Heat the oil, and sauté the onion and pepper until onion is translucent. Add flour, stirring constantly until flour is light brown. Add tomatoes, and gradually stir in the stock or wine, stirring until sauce thickens. Add lime juice and vinegar. Taste, and add salt and pepper as needed, and as much hot pepper sauce as you like.

MAKES ABOUT 2 CUPS

🎵 Sour-Cream Horseradish Sauce

Of Hungarian origin, this sauce is splendid for beef dishes. It's also good as a dressing for vegetables.

½ cup hot water
1 medium-size horseradish root, grated (about ¾ cup)
3 tablespoons butter
2 tablespoons flour
½ cup hot beef or chicken broth
½ cup hot milk
1 teaspoon sugar
1 teaspoon salt
2 tablespoons white vinegar
freshly ground black pepper
½ cup sour cream

Pour the hot water over grated horseradish. Let stand for 2 minutes to bring out the flavor, then drain and set aside. In a heavy pan over low heat, melt the butter, stir in flour, and let mixture bubble gently about 1 minute. Add the hot broth and milk all at once, stirring constantly until mixture forms a creamy sauce. Add sugar and salt. Simmer over very low heat for 5 minutes. Add horseradish, together with vinegar and pepper, and simmer for 12 minutes more. Adjust sweet/sour proportions to your taste, but keep sauce on the sour side. Just before serving, stir in sour cream. Serve at room temperature.

MAKES 2 CUPS

❧ Horseradish Sauce for Roast Beef

Traditional, as it deserves to be. There are many variations; this is one of the best.

> ½ cup freshly grated horseradish
> 1 cup mayonnaise (preferably homemade)
> 1 teaspoon dry mustard
> 1 teaspoon sugar
> 1 teaspoon white wine vinegar
> ¼ teaspoon salt
> ½ cup heavy cream, whipped, or ½ cup sour cream

In a mixing bowl, combine all ingredients except the cream. Blend well. Fold in the cream, gently but thoroughly. Chill for 1 hour.

MAKES ABOUT 2 CUPS

❧ Hot-and-Sweet Sauce

The conflict of sweet and hot flavors makes this an intriguing sauce to accompany cold roast meats or hot boiled beef.

> 3 tablespoons tarragon vinegar
> 4 tablespoons brown sugar
> 3 tablespoons dry mustard
> pinch salt

In a saucepan, heat the vinegar to a full, rolling boil. In a heat-proof bowl, mix sugar, mustard, and salt. Stir into it the boiling vinegar and blend thoroughly. Store in a tightly covered jar in the refrigerator for a few days before using. Serve cold.

MAKES ABOUT ½ CUP

🎵 Chinese Mustard

Always mix this zesty mustard just prior to use. Never save a leftover batch. I like flat beer best for this.

> ¼ cup dry mustard
> 3 or 4 tablespoons beer, sake, Japanese rice vinegar,
>   or water

Put mustard in a bowl or cup. Gradually add liquid, stirring until mixture is the consistency of heavy cream. Let mustard stand for 15 minutes to improve flavor.

MAKES ABOUT ¼ CUP

🎵 Hungarian Mustard Sauce

One of the most refreshing personalities in the food world is Chef Louis Szathmary, who, with his charming Japanese wife, operates The Bakery, a hugely successful Chicago restaurant. Once, when I asked Chef Louis why he thought Chicago was called the Second City, he replied: "Easy. There are more Hungarians in Boston than in Chicago."

This spicy sauce is good with Hungarian sausages, and of course with roast beef. It also makes an excellent sandwich spread in place of mayonnaise.

> 1 cup Bavarian mustard
> ⅓ cup white vinegar
> ⅛ teaspoon white pepper
> ¼ teaspoon salt
> ⅓ cup cornstarch
> ¼ cup Madeira, port, or cream sherry

Combine 1 quart water, ½ cup mustard, the vinegar, pepper, and salt in a saucepan. Bring to a boil over high heat, and stir with a wire whisk for about 1 minute.

Mix cornstarch with 1 cup water and slowly pour mixture

into boiling liquid, stirring constantly. Lower heat to medium and cook until mixture is thick, smooth, and opaque. Remove from heat and cool for 10 minutes, stirring occasionally. Stir in remaining ½ cup mustard and the wine; cool to room temperature and then chill. If refrigerated it will keep 2 to 3 weeks.

MAKES ABOUT 2 QUARTS

ஜ Devil Paste

A spicy sauce to serve with grilled steaks, lamb chops, kidneys, and even fish, if you like.

    2 teaspoons Major Grey chutney
    2 teaspoons Dijon mustard
    1 rounded teaspoon butter, softened
    1 teaspoon white vinegar
    generous dash lime juice
    large dash cayenne
    dash salt

If the chutney has lumps, mince them. Mix all ingredients until they make a smooth paste. Serve at room temperature.

MAKES APPROXIMATELY ½ CUP,
OR SERVINGS FOR 2

ஜ Hot-Hot Mustard Sauce

Frankly fiery but delectable, a special friend to rare roast beef. It can also be added discreetly to some salad dressings.

    1 teaspoon dry mustard
    pinch salt
    generous grinding black pepper
    ½ cup olive oil
    ½ teaspoon sugar
    1 teaspoon white wine vinegar, if needed

Into a chilled metal bowl put the mustard, salt, and pepper. Dribble the oil in slowly, beating briskly with a wire whisk, until the mixture becomes a fluffy mayonnaise. Add the sugar, and whisk again to mix well. If the sauce threatens to break down, beat in the vinegar.

MAKES ½ CUP

🎵 Hot Peanut Butter Sauce

This very hot dipping sauce is served with Indonesian Saté (see recipe). There are several variations, including the African. I like this Indonesian version best. Sambal oelik, a traditional, fiery Indonesian spice, is sold in exotic spice shops or obtainable by mail order.

Saté goes well with Pilaf (p. 169) and/or sambals. (Sambals are any mixture you wish of pickles, coconut, chopped peanuts, or pickled vegetables.)

> 1 tablespoon butter
> 1 small onion, grated
> 2 rounded tablespoons chunky peanut butter
> 1 tablespoon soy sauce
> 1 teaspoon lemon juice
> 1 rounded teaspoon sambal oelik or a mixture of the
>   following:
>   1 teaspoon soy sauce
>   1 teaspoon peanut oil
>   1 teaspoon dried red pepper flakes
> ½ cup milk

Heat butter in a heavy pan, and sauté onion until it begins to brown. Add the peanut butter, 1 tablespoon soy sauce, lemon juice, and sambal oelik or substitute mixture. Mix well. While continuing to stir, slowly add the milk to make a creamy sauce. Bring to a boil. This sauce should be served hot; if you make it in advance, reheat it almost to a boil just before serving.

When served with Indonesian Saté, a bowl of hot peanut

butter sauce is passed and each guest takes a spoonful. (It is a
rich sauce, and one spoonful is usually plenty.) Dip each bite
of meat into sauce.

MAKES ABOUT 1 CUP

ℜ Chimchurri and Piri-Piri
Two Frankly Fiery Sauces

Piri-piri is much used in Portuguese cooking. In Portuguese
Africa it is known as *jindungo*. Portuguese Brazilians also call
for piri-piri, but there is another Brazilian bit of hellfire they
love to daub on their steaks known as *chimchurri*. Piri-piri is
(are) a kind of pepper. I suspect *chimchurri* is an Indian word.
Guests should be warned not to overdo use of these smoking
liquids, which are delightful for perking up eggs, fish, broiled
chicken, grilled meats, or to give a lift to rice, plantains, or
other bland vegetables.

Piri-Piri 1
¼ cup seeded and minced dried red peppers
2 tablespoons white vinegar
2 tablespoons gin

Blend and let sit a few days in airtight bottle.

Piri-Piri 2
¼ cup seeded and minced fresh hot red peppers
1 cup olive oil
1 bay leaf
1 slice lemon rind

Combine ingredients and seal in airtight bottle. It keeps forever
at room temperature, and should be aged for 1 month before
using the first time.

Chimchurri
2 cherry peppers, minced
½ cup lemon juice
¼ cup peanut oil
2 tablespoons minced onion
2 tablespoons chopped fresh parsley

Combine ingredients and store in an airtight bottle.

This is especially good with grilled meats. It is not as blistering as piri-piri, and since it needs no aging, it can be made up and used immediately.

🎄 Berber and Taureg Basting Oil

Typically very fiery and yet with a dash of sweet, this goes well with barbecued meats, a couscous (p. 152), or a chicken dish. Ras el Hanout, which means "top of the shop"—or a little bit of everything—is a complex North African spice mixture that makes a curry powder seem simple. We approximate it in this recipe. Measurements are also "to taste": we offer only a suggested ratio.

5 tablespoons butter, softened
⅔ cup peanut oil
1 teaspoon Ras el Hanout (p. 15) or:
    ½ teaspoon curry powder (p. 13)
    ¼ teaspoon crushed basil
    ¼ teaspoon marjoram
    ¼ teaspoon powdered allspice
    ¼ teaspoon dried red pepper flakes
1 tablespoon ground peanuts or almonds
generous pinch freshly chopped mint
1 teaspoon honey
juice of 1 lemon
1 heaping tablespoon raisins

Mix all ingredients except lemon juice and raisins. Soak the raisins in lemon juice for 15 minutes, or until raisins are soft and plump. Stir into main mixture and blend well. Use sparingly.

MAKES ABOUT 1 CUP

ℵ Harissa
North African Hot Sauce

Harissa is the indispensable hot sauce (and it *is* hot!) used in many parts of North Africa for spicing up a couscous. It will also add a zip to cooked green vegetables, if used with caution. This is one version you can make at home. Definitely not for faint palates.

> 3 cloves garlic
> ½ teaspoon cayenne
> ½ teaspoon powdered cumin
> ½ teaspoon coriander seed
> ½ cup olive oil
> salt and freshly ground black pepper

In a mortar or a blender mash the garlic with the cayenne, cumin, coriander, and olive oil. Blend thoroughly. Add salt and pepper to taste. Pass this in a small serving bowl with couscous, so guests can hot up their plates to individual tastes.

MAKES ABOUT ½ CUP

ℵ Pepper Sherry

A dash of this elixir makes an exciting addition to salad dressings, meats, scrambled eggs, or whatever appeals to you. Use sparingly—it's potent.

    enough dried red peppers to fill an 8-ounce bottle or jar
    generous grinding black pepper
    generous squirt fresh lime juice
    pinch dry mustard
    enough dry Spanish sherry to fill the bottle (about
      6 ounces)

Fill a small clean bottle or jar with the hottest little red peppers you can find. Add the other ingredients, filling to top with the sherry last. Close the lid tightly and shake well to blend. Let the bottle stand, shaking it once a day, for about 3 weeks before you begin to use it. (If you miss a day, don't worry.)

    Replenish with good dry sherry as it is used, until the peppers have given their all.

SHOULD BE A YEAR'S SUPPLY

🎗 Sauce Vinaigrette

Every serious cook has a secret version of this classic dressing for salads, artichokes, mushrooms, and all the vegetables that taste good served cold. Now you have my secret. This vinaigrette will keep well in the refrigerator, but it will ensure your reputation as a vinaigrette aficionado if you make it just minutes before you use it.

    1 scant teaspoon Pommery or Dijon mustard
    1 tablespoon white wine vinegar
    generous pinch fresh herbs, such as tarragon or
      marjoram
    ½ teaspoon salt
    3 tablespoons fine olive oil
    freshly ground black pepper

Put mustard, vinegar, herbs, and salt in a small bowl. Mix thoroughly with a fork, scraping the bottom as you stir. Continue to whip, and dribble in the olive oil. Use your peppermill generously. If you refrigerate the dressing, stir-whip thoroughly again just before pouring over fresh, crisp salad greens.

MAKES ABOUT ¼ CUP

✿ Piquant Salad Dressing

With a bit of searching and a touch of imagination, it is possible to find fresh salad greens all year round. What a pity to use bottled salad dressing on them, when you can make a better one yourself.

    3 eggs
    1 tablespoon dry mustard
    1 tablespoon sugar
    2 cups olive oil
    ¾ cup white wine vinegar
    1 tablespoon garlic, minced
    juice of 1 lemon
    1 tablespoon A-1 sauce
    2 tablespoons Worcestershire sauce
    ½ teaspoon Tabasco
    1 tablespoon good chili powder
    ½ teaspoon salt
    freshly ground black pepper
    1 cup chopped watercress
    ½ cup chopped fresh parsley

Break the eggs into a large mixing bowl. Beat until foamy with a wire whisk. Add mustard and sugar, and mix well. Add olive oil slowly, beating constantly. When mixture is thick and smooth, blend in the vinegar, garlic, lemon juice, A-1 sauce, Worcestershire sauce, Tabasco, and chili powder. Mix well, and add salt and pepper. Stir in the watercress and parsley.

    Pour into a screw-cap jar, refrigerate, and use as needed. This salad dressing will keep 1 or 2 weeks if refrigerated.

MAKES 3 CUPS

✿ North African Salad Dressing

Oddly enough, this piquant dressing goes well with fruit salads and cottage cheese. A colorful and appropriate salad would be one made by alternating slices of tomatoes, onions, cucumbers, and bell pepper rings. A handsome party dish.

> ¾ cup olive oil
> ¼ cup fresh lemon juice
> 2 cloves garlic, minced
> 1½ teaspoons salt
> 3 dashes Tabasco
> 1 teaspoon sugar
> ½ teaspoon powdered coriander
> ½ teaspoon powdered cumin
> ½ teaspoon dry mustard
> ½ teaspoon Hungarian paprika

Put all ingredients in a jar with a tight-fitting lid. Shake well, and refrigerate a few hours before using.

MAKES 1 CUP

🎨 Spanish Salad Dressing

They may never have heard of this dressing in Spain, but in such good restaurants in New York City as El Faro and El Parador the house dressing is a cousin to the following. It has enough piquancy to make diners sit up and take notice of their food, even after one-more-than-necessary preprandial margarita.

> 1 cup olive oil
> ½ cup red wine vinegar
> ⅔ cup catsup
> 1 tablespoon Louisiana Hot Sauce, or 1 teaspoon Tabasco
> 2 teaspoons salt
> 1 teaspoon Hungarian paprika
> ½ onion, minced
> 2 cloves garlic, minced
> ½ teaspoon dry mustard
> ½ teaspoon confectioners' sugar
> freshly ground black pepper to taste

Put all ingredients in a blender and blend thoroughly. If mixing by hand, drip oil into vinegar, stirring constantly. Add all other ingredients and beat well with a wire whisk. Will keep indefinitely if refrigerated.

MAKES ABOUT 2 CUPS

🎵 Salsa Fuerte
Texas Salad Dressing

Salsa fuerte, translated literally, means "strong sauce." This is a pungent dressing that I sometimes serve over salad greens when I have a *bravo* for a guest. It's a mixture that does triple duty as a dressing for meats and vegetables as well as salads.

To use salsa fuerte with meats, mix all ingredients and sauté for 3 minutes over a high flame. Add 2 cups good chicken broth. Simmer and reduce until sauce thickens. This makes an excellent sauce for Latin meats and vegetables.

   4 tomatoes, chopped
   1 small onion, minced
   2 stalks celery, finely chopped
   ½ cup ground almonds
   2 tablespoons fine olive oil
   1 dried red pepper, seeded and minced, or ½ teaspoon
      cayenne
   1 sprig parsley, chopped
   1 rounded teaspoon authentic chili powder
   ½ teaspoon salt

Mix all ingredients well, chill, and serve over salad greens.

MAKES ABOUT 1 CUP

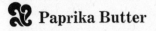 Paprika Butter

A lively and versatile seasoning to be spread over meat, poultry, or fish before broiling, or added by the tablespoon to cooked vegetables.

¼ pound (1 stick) butter
1 teaspoon Hungarian paprika
1 teaspoon lemon juice
¼ teaspoon salt
freshly ground black pepper to taste

Combine all ingredients in a mixing bowl. Blend thoroughly, and let stand at room temperature for at least 30 minutes so flavors can meld.

MAKES ABOUT ½ CUP

 Spicy Vegetable Butter

Here's an excellent seasoned butter. This one is guaranteed to perk up almost any fresh, cooked vegetable.

3 tablespoons butter
¼ teaspoon Hungarian paprika
dash freshly grated nutmeg
dash cayenne

Combine all ingredients and mix well. Stir into cooked vegetables just before serving.

ENOUGH FOR VEGETABLES
FOR 4

🎱 Lime Pepper Butter

Attractive to the eye as well as to the plate, this will adorn a chop, but goes especially well with grilled fish.

½ pound (2 sticks) butter
juice of 1 lime
cayenne to taste

Soften the butter in a shallow bowl. Add lime juice and cream well. Tilt plate to let surplus juice run off. Mix in cayenne. When thoroughly blended, smooth and reshape into a flat square. Chill until firm. Using a butter curler, or working carefully with the blade of a chilled knife, take off curls of chilled butter. Keep each curl firm by placing it on ice. Place one butter curl on top of each chop or slice of fish just before it is served.

MAKES 1 CUP

Breads

꧄ Biscuits or Biscuit Crust

What a boon to waken to the smell of bacon frying, coffee in the making, and knowing that fresh biscuits will soon be ready for a dripping of butter or a smear of golden honey. This recipe makes biscuits, or a biscuit crust to top meat pies, depending on how you cut it. Nothing spicy here, but a useful basic for many recipes. Do not twist the cutter when stamping out the biscuits—they will not rise well.

1 cup flour
2 teaspoons baking powder
dash salt
¼ pound (1 stick) butter or margarine
about ¼ cup milk or ice water

Sift dry ingredients into a bowl. Cut the butter or margarine into small dabs, and work it into flour mixture with two knives or a pastry blender to create a mix that looks like peas in size. Add milk or ice water, a dribble at a time, stirring with a fork. *Use just enough liquid to hold the dough together—the less used, the better.*

Work the dough into a ball. Lightly flour a board and roll out the dough to a thickness of about ½ inch.

To make biscuits, stamp out in 2- or 3-inch circles, and refrigerate (if you can spare the time) for an hour, to rest the dough. Bake on ungreased cookie sheet for 12 minutes at 450° F.

To make a crust, roll into a circle bigger than the pie. Wipe rolling pin with flour, and roll up crust onto pin. Then unroll crust onto pie, trim, and bake in preheated 275° F. oven for 20 to 30 minutes.

For a more down-home flavor use buttermilk, reduce baking powder to 1 teaspoon, and add ¾ teaspoon baking soda.

MAKES 10 BISCUITS
OR 1 CRUST

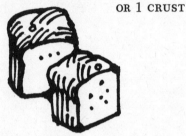

𝒜 Devil Biscuits

These little snacks will make the drinks taste better. They can be served plain, fresh from the oven, or decorated with anchovy butter or any other savory topping.

> 1 cup flour
> ¼ pound butter
> 2 teaspoons baking powder
> 1 teaspoon salt
> ¼ teaspoon freshly ground white pepper
> 1 small dried red pepper, seeded and minced, or
>   pinch cayenne
> about ¼ cup water

Preheat oven to 350° F. Put all ingredients except water in a mixing bowl and blend with two knives, or a pastry cutter, until mealy. Add just enough water to bind, and mix well into a soft ball of dough. Pat or roll out into a 1-inch-thick sheet on floured board. Do not knead more than necessary. Cut into 2-inch rounds with small drinking glass—stamping out biscuits with no twisting motion. Bake on an ungreased baking sheet for 12 minutes.

MAKES ABOUT 16 BISCUITS

ஜ Ginger Biscuits

Served piping hot, these snappy biscuits go nicely with an after-noon cup of tea or coffee.

   1 cup flour
   2 teaspoons baking powder
   ½ cup sugar
   1 tablespoon powdered ginger
   ¼ pound butter
   1 egg
   about ¼ cup milk

Heat oven to 350° F. Mix flour, baking powder, sugar, and gin-ger together, then cut the butter in with two knives until the mixture becomes mealy. Beat the egg well and add to mixture to form dough. Moisten with just enough milk to make the dough hold together. Knead very little; patting into shape is better. Pat or roll out into a ½-inch-thick sheet on a floured board. Stamp out biscuits, and bake on an ungreased baking sheet for about 12 minutes, until golden.

MAKES ABOUT 10 BISCUITS

ஜ Hungarian Pepper Biscuits

A most unusual biscuit. If you punch these out in a small size, they make a nice accompaniment for a glass of red wine or a cup of homemade soup.

   ½ pound butter
   2 cups flour
   3 teaspoons baking powder
   ½ teaspoon salt
   1 teaspoon freshly ground black pepper
   3 medium-size cooked potatoes, mashed, about 1 cup
   1 egg yolk
   1 teaspoon water

Blend butter, flour, baking powder, salt, and pepper to form a crumbly mixture. Add mashed potatoes and knead very quickly— do not work for more than a few minutes. Roll out dough on a floured board; fold it once. Chill for 30 minutes.

Repeat kneading, rolling, and chilling twice more.

Heat the oven to 375° F. Roll out dough to 1-inch thickness and cut into rounds. Crisscross tops of biscuits with a knife point. Beat egg yolk with the water; brush on biscuits to glaze tops. Place on ungreased baking sheet, and bake for about 20 minutes, until biscuits are a shiny gold color but not brown.

MAKES 18 TO 24 BISCUITS

🎵 Fluffy Dumplings

A delicate dumpling to complement a spicy soup or stew. Follow these directions carefully, and your dumpling will be positively ethereal.

For even fluffier dumplings, drop by spoonfuls into *gently* bubbling soup or stew. Turn heat down to simmer and cook for 10 minutes. Cover tightly and simmer 10 minutes longer.

1 egg
¾ cup milk
2 cups presifted flour
3 teaspoons baking powder
½ teaspoon salt
1 tablespoon butter, melted

In a mixing bowl, beat the egg, then add milk and beat again. Sift together the flour, baking powder, and salt. Gradually stir flour mixture into egg mixture. Add butter and stir again to mix well. Drop by spoonfuls into simmering water or soup. Cover and cook about 10 minutes.

MAKES 12 DUMPLINGS

❧ Hungarian-Style Little Dumplings

These fluffy balls go well with a host of stews and soups.

    2 eggs
    6 tablespoons flour
    pinch salt

Mix eggs, flour, and salt. Spoon out mixture ¼ teaspoon at a time and drop into boiling soup or other liquid, and cover. These tiny dumplings will cook in about 3 minutes. Serve at once.

SERVES 4

❧ Chili Cornbread

Goes well with fried fish or a juicy baked ham. If you can't find jalapeño peppers, use double the amount of regular green chilies, fresh or canned.

    1 tablespoon bacon fat, lard, or butter
    1 cup cornmeal
    ½ cup sifted flour
    1 teaspoon salt
    1 teaspoon baking soda
    ½ teaspoon sugar
    2 eggs
    1 onion, chopped
    3 jalapeño peppers, chopped
    ¼ pound cheddar cheese, grated
    1 cup buttermilk
    ⅓ cup olive oil

Heat oven to 450° F. Grease an 8-inch iron skillet with bacon fat, lard, or butter. In a large bowl, mix cornmeal, flour, salt, baking soda, and sugar. In a separate bowl, beat eggs lightly and add onion, peppers, and cheese. Stir, add buttermilk and olive oil, and mix well. Combine egg mixture with dry ingredients and mix thoroughly. Pour into skillet and bake for 20 minutes, until lightly golden.

SERVES 4 TO 6

🎵 Sour-Cream Chili Cornbread

This is spicy for a cornbread, but it makes a mild accompaniment to any Mexican meal or a barbecue.

    2 eggs
    13-ounce can cream-style corn
    1 cup sour cream
    ¼ pound (1 stick) butter, melted
    1 cup coarse cornmeal
    1 teaspoon salt
    1 teaspoon baking powder
    ¼ pound Monterey Jack or cheddar cheese, grated
    8-ounce can green chilies, drained

Preheat oven to 375° F. Beat the eggs. Add the corn, sour cream, and butter, and blend. Mix cornmeal, salt, and baking powder together. Combine the dry ingredients with the wet. Stir in the cheese. Pour into a buttered 9-inch square pan, stopping when you have poured in half the mix. Now lay the green chilies carefully to make stripes across the batter. Carefully add the remainder of the batter. Bake for 40 minutes, or until cornbread is golden.

SERVES 4

🎵 Easy Saffron Bread

Originating in the East and introduced into Spain by the Arabs, saffron is more expensive than gold, and similarly unique.

1 cup milk
3 tablespoons sugar
2 tablespoons butter
2 teaspoons minced onion
⅛ teaspoon saffron threads, crushed
2 teaspoons salt
2 packages dry yeast
1 cup warm water
4½ cups all-purpose flour
sprinkling caraway seed

Scald milk, remove from heat, and stir in sugar, butter, onion, saffron, and salt. Cool to lukewarm. In a large mixing bowl, sprinkle yeast over warm water. Stir until yeast is dissolved, then add milk mixture. Add flour; stir until well blended. Cover and set in warm place. Let rise to more than double in bulk (about 40 minutes).

Heat oven to 375° F. Stir batter down and beat vigorously for about 30 seconds. Turn into greased 1½-quart round casserole. Sprinkle top lightly with caraway seed. Bake for about 20 minutes.

MAKES 1 LOAF

🎵 Sicilian Pepper Cheese Bread

Something different to serve with pasta, or any hearty peasant casserole.

1 loaf crusty Italian bread
⅓ cup olive oil
⅔ cup grated Romano or Parmesan cheese
freshly ground black pepper

Preheat oven to 400° F. Slice loaf in half lengthwise. Brush both halves with the oil, and sprinkle with the grated cheese and grindings of pepper. (Make sure you *see* the pepper!) Place on

baking sheet or wrap in foil and bake until cheese is melted
(about 10 minutes). Cut into thick slices and serve while still
piping hot.

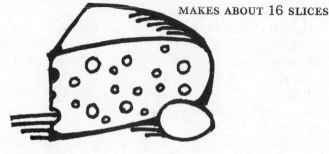

MAKES ABOUT 16 SLICES

🐾 Garlic Cheese Bread

With almost all pasta dishes and many casseroles a good crusty
herb or garlic bread is indispensable. If you are lucky enough to
have sourdough bread available, use it by all means. Otherwise,
seek the crustiest, toughest, least cottony bread you can obtain.

 1 crusty loaf French or Italian bread
 ⅓ cup grated cheddar, asiago, or other cheese to your
  liking
 ¼ pound (1 stick) butter, softened
 2 cloves garlic, mashed

Heat oven to 350° F. Slice the loaf of bread in half the long way.
Make three deep slashes the length of the loaf in each half,
taking care not to cut the bread all the way through. Sprinkle
grated cheese generously into the slashes. Cream butter with
garlic, and spread a thin layer of garlic butter on the cut surface
of each half. Squeeze the loaf together. Now, slice the loaf almost through, crosswise, in slices about 2 inches wide. Bread will
end up in rough cubes. Encase the loaf in foil wrap. Heat in oven
for about 15 minutes, until cheese is melted. Do not serve lukewarm—if need be, wait until all plates are full and then pass
this beautiful bread hot as hot can be.

SERVES 6 TO 8

∾ Jalapeño Hush Puppies

Yes, this deep-fried cornbread *was* devised to keep hungry dogs quiet. It originated at an old-time Southern fish fry; authentic hush puppies, therefore, should contain fish cracklings, and never jalapeños. Let's just say this recipe comes from the South— of Texas. The formula will produce light, fluffy puppies with a special tang.

    2 cups cornmeal
    2 cups cream-style corn
    ½ cup flour
    2 eggs, beaten
    3 teaspoons baking powder
    1½ teaspoons salt
    3 jalapeño peppers or fresh green chilies, chopped
    ½ bell pepper, chopped
    1 small onion, minced
    large pinch baking soda
    about ½ cup buttermilk
    3 cups lard or vegetable oil

Mix all ingredients except lard or oil, using enough buttermilk to make a creamy batter. In a deep pot, heat fat to 375° F. Test your batter by spooning off a bit into the hot fat. If it seems heavy, add another pinch of baking powder. If it is greasy and breaks up, add a little more flour. (And for more zip, add some jalapeño pepper juice!) Drop batter, by the tablespoon, into hot fat. When puppies are golden brown—about 5 minutes—drain and place on paper towel. Serve on a warmed plate.

MAKES ABOUT 30, OR
ENOUGH TO HUSH 6 PUPPIES

Desserts

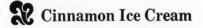 Champagne Sundae

Following a rich dinner, something small, cool, yet lively is often what is needed. This dessert is simple, always a hit, and it doesn't take much champagne. Be sure the champagne is of good quality, the glasses chilled.

    1 quart lemon ice
    8 teaspoons crème de menthe
    ½ bottle champagne

Fill 8 parfait glasses with lemon ice, near to brim. With a spoon or your forefinger, drill a small hole in the center of each mound of ice. Fill each hole with 1 teaspoon crème de menthe. As the liquid disperses, top with the champagne.

SERVES 8

Cinnamon Ice Cream

Here's a simple way to "specialize" dessert for unexpected guests. It's good as is, and delightful with warm Spicy Apple Pie (see recipe).

1 quart vanilla ice cream
1 rounded teaspoon powdered cinnamon

Let ice cream soften just enough to stir. Add cinnamon and mix thoroughly. Spoon into freezer tray and immediately refreeze.

SERVES 4

Persimmon Pudding

Persimmons are among the most beautiful of all fruits. We have persimmon pudding and hard sauce every year during the holidays. The dish has much of the taste of good plum pudding without all the calories (of course, you must measure your hard sauce carefully).

1 cup sugar
1 cup flour
pulp from 2 large persimmons, to make 1 cup
½ cup milk
1 level teaspoon baking soda
1 tablespoon butter, melted
½ teaspoon powdered cinnamon
½ teaspoon freshly grated nutmeg
½ teaspoon powdered allspice
½ teaspoon powdered coriander (optional)
1 teaspoon vanilla
½ teaspoon salt
Hard Sauce (following recipe) or whipped cream

Preheat oven to 350° F. Thoroughly mix all ingredients except hard sauce or whipped cream. Bake in a covered dish for 1 hour.
Serve with hard sauce or whipped cream.

SERVES 6 TO 8

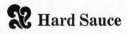 Hard Sauce

There are many variations, but this one is my favorite. It goes beautifully with pumpkin or mince pie, or plum or persimmon pudding.

  1 cup confectioners' sugar
  ¼ pound (1 stick) butter, softened
  3 tablespoons cream
  ½ teaspoon vanilla
  1 teaspoon fine Cognac
  dusting of cinnamon

Beat the sugar into the softened butter. Add the milk or cream, vanilla, and Cognac and keep beating (with electric beater or wire whisk) until mixture is smooth and velvety. Put in serving bowl and dust top with a circle of cinnamon. Chill before serving.

MAKES ABOUT 1½ CUPS

Goldie's Ginger Dandies

These little snappers were so elegant they were originally made to be sold exclusively in that high-fashion establishment, Henri Bendel. For a considerable bribe, their creator, Goldie Blanksteen, agreed to share her gold with us.

  ½ pound (2 sticks) butter, at room temperature
  ½ cup sugar plus more for rolling cookies
  ⅜ cup molasses
  ½ teaspoon vanilla
  1 tablespoon powdered ginger
  1 teaspoon freshly grated nutmeg
  3 cups flour
  1½ teaspoons baking soda
  ⅛ teaspoon salt

Cream the softened butter and ½ cup sugar, adding sugar gradually. Gradually beat in the molasses and add the vanilla. Combine all the other ingredients and stir into the sugar-butter to form a dough.

Place plastic wrap on a tray or baking sheet, put dough on top, and cover with a second layer of plastic. Flatten dough with a rolling pin until it is 1 inch thick. Chill at least 1 hour.

Preheat oven to 375° F. Uncover and cut the dough into 1-inch squares. Roll each square into a ball, then roll balls into sugar to coat. Place cookies on ungreased baking sheet, ½ inch apart. Flatten each ball slightly with a fork. Bake 12 to 15 minutes until lightly browned. Let cookies cool on the baking sheet.

MAKES ABOUT 60 COOKIES

ℜ Brandied Ginger Balls

Bake these delicious cookies a few days before the holiday rush; they'll keep well for unexpected guests.

  ½ pound (2 sticks) butter, softened
  ½ cup brown sugar
  ½ cup molasses
  2 tablespoons brandy or dry sherry
  2 cups unbleached flour
  1½ teaspoons powdered ginger
  ½ teaspoon freshly grated nutmeg
  ½ teaspoon salt
  ½ cup confectioners' sugar, as needed

Preheat oven to 300° F. Grease baking sheet. Cream together butter, brown sugar, molasses, and brandy or sherry. Sift together flour, ginger, nutmeg, and salt, and sift again into butter-sugar mixture. Mix well, and form into walnut-size balls. Place on greased cookie sheet and bake for 15 minutes. Remove cookies to a platter and, while they are still warm, sift confectioners' sugar over all. When cool, sift more sugar over them. Store in a cool place.

MAKES ABOUT 40 COOKIES

❦ Peppercorn Cookies

I have never been able to learn the origin of these peppery delights. One educated guess is that they might be Hungarian. Whatever the source, they are unique in taste—and just wait for that afterbite! One caution: You *must* use freshly cracked pepper for this recipe.

  3 cups all-purpose flour, sifted
  2 teaspoons double-acting baking powder
  ½ pound (2 sticks) butter, softened
  1 generous teaspoon freshly cracked peppercorns
  pinch cayenne
  1 tablespoon powdered ginger
  2 teaspoons powdered cinnamon
  ½ teaspoon powdered cloves
  1¾ cups sugar
  1 egg

Preheat oven to 400° F. Sift flour and baking powder together into a bowl. In another large mixing bowl, cream the butter with an electric beater until it is pale yellow and fluffy. Beat in the pepper, cayenne, ginger, cinnamon, cloves, and sugar. Add egg, beating at lowest speed and scraping bowl to keep the mixture well blended. Add the sifted flour, still scraping to keep mixture smooth. Remove dough to lightly floured surface and knead a few times.

Divide the dough into three equal portions. With a lightly floured rolling pin, roll one portion of dough at a time until it is about ⅛ inch thick. Cut into cookie shapes. Transfer cookies to an ungreased cookie sheet, spacing them ¾ inch apart. Bake about 12 minutes, or until edges turn brown. If you use more than one cookie sheet, be sure to reverse position of cookies during cooking. Baking time will also be a little longer. Cool on a rack.

MAKES ABOUT 36 COOKIES

ℜ Pastry for a One- or Two-Crust Pie (9-Inch)

This piecrust recipe, enough for a 9-inch pie pan, is easy—and it works. For a one-crust pie, use half the recipe.

2¼ cups all-purpose flour, sifted
1 teaspoon salt
¾ cup shortening (half and half butter and lard suggested)
5 or 6 tablespoons ice water

In a mixing bowl combine flour and salt. With pastry blender, or using two knives, cut in shortening until mixture becomes a coarse meal.

One tablespoon at a time, add water and mix with a fork, lightly, until all flour is moistened and becomes a doughy mass. Gather dough into a bowl. Place in a plastic bag and chill for at least 30 minutes. Divide dough in half and roll out each part separately. Try picking up rolled-out dough by rolling it up on rolling pin and then unrolling it onto pie tin. Flute edges with fingers or crimp with fork.

For a prebaked shell, heat oven to 425° F. Fit crust into pie plate, prick sides and bottom with a fork. Bake 12 to 15 minutes until golden. Cool before filling.

ℜ Shortcut Mince Pie

While I admire cooks who begin from scratch in everything, I confess I sometimes use shortcuts for convenience. Of course, the shortcuts must involve quality materials. If you have the time, by all means begin your pie with source materials; however, follow this recipe and your friends will probably cry: "Home-made!" But, be sure to use *fresh* lemon juice only.

1 or more jars prepared mincemeat (about 3 cups)
2 cups peeled, cubed apples (preferably Granny Smiths)
1 cup seedless raisins
1 cup water
1 tablespoon fresh lemon juice
2 tablespoons flour
½ cup sugar
pastry for 2-crust 9-inch pie (see preceding recipe)

Preheat oven to 350° F. In a saucepan, combine mincemeat, apples, raisins, water, and lemon juice. Combine flour and sugar. Stir this into the mincemeat mixture. Bring mixture to boil, stirring constantly. Empty into an uncooked pie shell. Roll out second pastry crust and slice into ½-inch lattice strips. Crisscross over top of pie, turn up bottom edges, and seal. With fork or thumb, crimp edges.

Bake pie about 50 minutes, until crust is golden brown. Set on rack to cool.

SERVES 6 TO 8

ℬ Spicy Apple Pie

Traditional with a twist, this apple pie has a bit more zing than most. I like to use Granny Smith apples for this one. It's an open-face pie, but there is no reason why you can't make it with a top crust.

1 cup light-brown sugar, packed
½ cup all-purpose flour
¼ pound (1 stick) butter
½ teaspoon grated lemon peel
1 teaspoon powdered cinnamon
⅛ teaspoon powdered allspice
⅛ teaspoon powdered cloves
⅛ teaspoon freshly grated nutmeg
pastry for 1-crust 9-inch pie (p. 270)
7 or 8 medium cooking applies, peeled, cored, and sliced

Preheat oven to 400° F. Mix sugar, flour, butter, lemon peel, and spices with a pastry blender until they are crumbly. Spread a third of this mixture over bottom of unbaked pastry shell. Arrange apple slices on top. Spoon the rest of the sugar and spice mixture over apples. Bake for 50 to 60 minutes, until crust is golden brown.

SERVES 6 TO 8

𝕬 Spicy Louisiana Yam Pie

There is nothing unusual about this dessert except that it is mouth-watering, and not served often enough by us Northerners.

    3 or 4 yams, cooked, about 1½ cups
    ½ cup sugar
    1 teaspoon powdered cinnamon
    1 teaspoon powdered allspice
    ½ teaspoon salt
    3 eggs
    1 cup milk
    2 tablespoons butter, melted
    pastry for 1-crust 9-inch pie (p. 270)

Preheat oven to 350° F. Mash yams until free of lumps. Add sugar, cinnamon, allspice, and salt. In a separate bowl, beat eggs and add to mixture. Cream well. Blend milk and butter. Add to mixture and blend well. Pour into pastry shell. Bake 40 to 50 minutes or until a knife inserted in the center comes out clean.

SERVES 6 TO 8

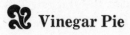 Vinegar Pie

This is a classic from the prairies; it tastes surprisingly close to lemon pie.

 1 cup sugar
 3 tablespoons flour
 ¼ teaspoon freshly grated nutmeg
 ¾ cup water
 2 tablespoons cider vinegar
 2 large eggs, beaten
 ⅓ cup butter, melted
 pastry for 1-crust 9-inch pie (p. 270)

Preheat oven to 350° F. Blend sugar, flour, and nutmeg until well mixed. Stir in water, vinegar, eggs, and butter, and beat only enough to mix well. Pour into pie shell and bake about 50 minutes, until filling is puffed and brown. Remove from oven and allow to cool before cutting—it will thicken as it cools.

SERVES 4 TO 6

 Spicy Pumpkin Pie

This is a creamy pumpkin pie that should not have to wait for Thanksgiving.

 1½ cups cooked pumpkin
 1 cup brown sugar, firmly packed
 1 heaping teaspoon freshly grated nutmeg
 1 heaping teaspoon powdered cinnamon
 1 teaspoon powdered allspice
 ½ teaspoon powdered ginger
 3 eggs, beaten
 13-ounce can evaporated milk
 pastry for 1-crust 9-inch pie (p. 270)

Preheat oven to 425° F. Combine pumpkin, sugar, nutmeg, cinnamon, allspice, and ginger. Add beaten eggs and mix well. Gradually stir in evaporated milk until mixture is thoroughly blended. Pour into pie shell.

Bake in 425° oven for 15 minutes. Reduce heat to 350° F. and bake 35 to 40 minutes, or until knife inserted in center comes out clean. Cool on rack.

Optional: When pie has cooled, top with whipped cream, or ¼ cup honey mixed with ¼ cup finely chopped pecans or walnuts.

SERVES 6 TO 8

℘ The Absolute Chocolate Pie

As a working chocaholic, I sample everything chocolaty I can get my mouth on. I have never found a recipe to match this one for the supernal chocolate pie. You can top with meringue and bake, or let cool and top with whipped cream.

        13-ounce can evaporated milk
        ⅔ cup finest cocoa obtainable (Droste, Bakers, or other fine
            brand)
        ¼ cup flour
        ¾ cup plus 3 tablespoons sugar
        ⅔ cup water
        ½ teaspoon salt
        2 eggs, separated
        1 teaspoon butter
        1½ teaspoons vanilla
        1 graham cracker crust (following recipe)
        ¼ teaspoon cream of tartar

In top of double boiler, heat the milk until very hot. Mix to a paste the cocoa, flour, ¾ cup sugar, water, and salt. Stir mixture into the hot milk. Stir continuously until thickened (this may take 15 minutes). Then cover and cook undisturbed for 5 minutes more. Remove from heat.

Meanwhile, separate eggs and beat yolks lightly—reserving

whites for meringue. When you remove pudding from heat, add 2 tablespoonfuls to the yolk mixture and blend. (This prevents eggs from curdling.) Now quickly stir the egg mixture back into the pudding, and stir in butter and 1 teaspoon vanilla. Let cool undisturbed. Pour pudding into pie shell, and make meringue.

Beat egg whites until foamy. Add cream of tartar. Beat until stiff but not dry, so that peaks lean slightly. Add 3 tablespoons sugar, 1 teaspoon at a time, beating after each addition. Add ½ teaspoon vanilla. Pour over pie, making sure meringue touches pie crust all around. Bake in preheated oven at 350° F. for 10 to 15 minutes, until meringue is golden. Let cool before cutting.

SERVES 6 TO 8

Spiced Graham Cracker Crust

1½ cups graham cracker crumbs (about 20 squares)
¼ cup butter, melted
¼ cup sugar
½ teaspoon powdered cinnamon
⅛ teaspoon freshly grated nutmeg

Preheat oven to 350° F. Roll crackers into crumbs on a sheet of waxed paper, using a rolling pin, or crush in a bowl. Mix all ingredients and put into a 9- or 10-inch pie pan. Press crust evenly over bottom and around sides of pan. Bake for 8 minutes. Cool before filling.

MAKES ONE 9-INCH PIECRUST

℀ Spiced Bavarian Cream

This variation on the classic dessert is light, rich, and irresistible.

  3½ cups milk
  2 envelopes unflavored gelatin
  6 eggs, separated
  ¾ cup sugar
  ¼ teaspoon salt
  ½ teaspoon powdered ginger
  ¼ teaspoon freshly grated nutmeg
  ⅛ teaspoon powdered cardamom
  1½ teaspoons vanilla
  1 cup heavy cream
  fresh berries or fruit, as desired

Scald 3 cups milk and soak gelatin in remaining ½ cup milk. Separate eggs. Beat together egg yolks, sugar, salt, ginger, nutmeg, and cardamom. Slowly add scalded milk to egg yolk mixture. Cook over double boiler, stirring constantly, until custard thickens enough to coat a silver spoon. Add softened gelatin, stirring until gelatin melts. Cool. Add vanilla and chill until slightly thickened. Meanwhile, beat egg whites until they are stiff, and whip cream. Now fold egg whites and whipped cream into custard, reserving 4 tablespoons of whipped cream. Spoon into 2½-quart mold or bowl. Chill until firm. Remove from mold and garnish with reserved whipped cream and/or fresh berries or fruit as desired.

SERVES 6

℀ New England Pork Cake

This cake can only be described as "robust." An excellent choice when houseguests are expected, since you can bake and refrigerate it two or three days before they arrive.

2 cups unbleached flour
1 teaspoon powdered cinnamon
½ teaspoon powdered ginger
¼ teaspoon powdered cloves
¼ teaspoon powdered allspice
½ pound salt pork, minced
½ cup dark molasses
¾ cup sugar
1 cup hot strong coffee
1 teaspoon baking soda
1 cup raisins
⅓ cup dry sherry, if needed

Preheat oven to 350° F. Sift together the flour, cinnamon, ginger, cloves, and allspice. Mix salt pork, molasses, sugar, coffee, and baking soda. Stir well, and add flour mixture. Fold in raisins.

Pour batter into a well-greased sheet-cake pan (11¾ by 7½ by 1¾ inches), and bake for 50 minutes, or until a toothpick inserted into the center comes out clean.

This will keep well if you sprinkle ⅓ cup sherry over the surface, then wrap the cake in waxed paper or plastic wrap and refrigerate.

SERVES 8 TO 10

Beverages

🎵 Café Brûlot

If you've ever dined at one of the famous restaurants in New Orleans, you probably finished a sumptuous meal with a café brûlot. Many are the recipes—this is one I like. You can create quite a spectacle if you cascade the flaming liquid from about a foot above the bowl. Better practice first.

    1 stick cinnamon
    6 whole cloves
    10 thin slivers orange peel
    10 thin slivers lemon peel
    3 small lumps sugar, or 1 rounded teaspoon sugar
    5 ounces good brandy
    1 ounce Curaçao
    1 quart strong black hot coffee

In a heated chafing dish, mix the cinnamon, cloves, orange and lemon peels, and sugar. Crush sugar lumps and stir. Add 4 ounces of the brandy and the ounce of Curaçao. Warm a large spoon over a flame. Remove the spoon from the heat and pour into it the remaining ounce of brandy. Carefully ignite the brandy by holding a lighted match to the edge of the spoon. Quickly pour the flaming brandy into the chafing dish and stir until the sugar dissolves. Gradually pour in the black coffee, continuing to stir as long as there is a blue flame. Serve in demitasse cups, with a bit of peel in each cup.

SERVES 10

𝄐 Coffee Grog

This once popular sturdy brew has, for some reason, lately fallen out of fashion. Too bad, for while it is not an everyday drink, it can be a great finale to a special party repast.

4 scant teaspoons brown sugar
1 teaspoon butter
⅛ teaspoon powdered cinnamon
⅛ teaspoon powdered cloves
⅛ teaspoon freshly grated nutmeg
6 ounces light rum
8 tablespoons cream
4 cups hot fresh coffee
4 thin strips orange peel
4 thin strips lemon peel

Preheat four ceramic mugs by filling with very hot water. Cream sugar, butter, and spices until they form a smooth mixture. Empty the mugs and add 1 rounded tablespoon of sugar mixture to each. Add, to each mug, 1½ ounces of rum and 2 tablespoons cream. Fill mugs with hot coffee, stir, garnish each with an orange and lemon peel, and serve at once.

SERVES 4

𝄐 Glögg

Pronounced *gloog*, this famous Swedish punch makes for a marvelous holiday spirit. We serve it at our Open House on New Year's Day. Glögg certainly warms the cockles.

4 whole cloves
1 stick cinnamon, crushed
2 whole cardamom pods, crushed
8 black peppercorns
2 cups water
¼ cup blanched almonds
½ cup white raisins
1 strip orange rind
2 bottles good Burgundy
1 bottle good port
sugar (optional)
akvavit, rum, or Cognac

Put cloves, cinnamon, cardamom, and peppercorns in a small cheesecloth bag and tie securely. Place in saucepan, add the water, and bring to boil. Lower heat and simmer until water is reduced to about half. Discard spices.

Add the almonds, raisins, orange rind, Burgundy, port, and a little sugar, if you wish. Bring quickly to a boil and remove from heat. Refrigerate, covered, to meld at least 12 hours.

To serve, reheat mixture and pour into thick, heated mugs. Top each mug with an ounce of akvavit, rum, or Cognac. Be sure each mug gets a few raisins and almonds.

SERVES 8 FREEZING PEOPLE OR
12 MODERATELY COLD PEOPLE

Hot Buttered Rum

This is a delicious brew for coming in out of the cold, or as a nightcap on a frosty evening. A pewter mug adds old-fashioned charm to the drink.

4 ounces dark Jamaica or Demerara rum
1 thin strip lemon peel
1 stick cinnamon
2 to 4 whole cloves
boiling cider
dab butter

In a warmed mug or a pewter tankard put rum, lemon peel, cinnamon stick, and cloves. Stirring with the cinnamon stick, fill mug with boiling cider. Float a dab of butter on the top, and do not stir it into the drink.

SERVES 1

🦋 Quentao
Brazilian Spiced Rum Punch

Here's a lovely and exotic surprise for guests invited on a cold winter's night.

    4 cups water
    1 pint good dark rum
    6 whole cloves
    1 vanilla bean, cut into thirds
    2 cups sugar
    2 thin quarter-size slices fresh ginger

In a pan with a tight-fitting lid, bring the water to a rolling boil. Add all the other ingredients. Remove from heat, stir, and cover. Let the mixture steep for 30 minutes, strain, and set aside. When guests arrive, reheat and serve piping hot in pottery mugs.

SERVES 8 TO 10

🦋 Hot Mulled Wine

An extremely simple recipe, but it can help a winter's evening pass cozily—particularly if you sip the mulled wine while sitting in easy chairs before a blazing fire. Warning: If you have more than one glass, don't expect to get out of your chair until the fire goes out.

    1 bottle good dry red table wine
    1 cup sugar
    1 teaspoon whole cloves
    1 short stick of cinnamon for each glass

Combine all ingredients and warm over a gentle flame, being careful not to boil. Warm glasses in hot water, dry quickly, and fill, making certain that each glass gets at least one clove and a cinnamon stick.

MAKES ABOUT 1 QUART

ℜ Bullshot

This has always seemed more like a soup than a drink to me. In some states where at certain times it is illegal to serve cocktails, I have had a Bloody Mary or a bullshot soup to start a meal.

    2 ounces gin or vodka
    1 teaspoon fresh lemon juice
    dash Worcestershire sauce
    hearty dash Tabasco
    ½ cup beef bouillon

Place all ingredients over ice in a mixer, adding bouillon last and to your taste. Mix well and strain into a highball or double-Manhattan glass.
Note: Half and half tomato juice and bouillon makes a Bloody Bullshot.

SERVES 1

ℜ Red Snapper Cocktail
The Original Bloody Mary

Every popular cocktail has its legion claiming they devised the original. The famed St. Regis–Sheraton Hotel in Manhattan is firm in its insistence that the original Bloody Mary was born from their Red Snapper. With their permission, the original original recipe appears below.

2 ounces vodka
2 ounces tomato juice
dash lemon juice
dash cayenne
dash salt
dash Worcestershire sauce

Mix all ingredients with cracked ice in a shaker. Shake well and serve on the rocks.

SERVES 1

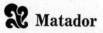 Matador

The Mexican Bloody Mary. It is also known as a Bloody Maria.

4 ounces tomato juice
2 ounces tequila
juice of ½ lime
dash Tabasco
dash Worcestershire sauce
small dash salt
freshly ground black pepper to taste

Mix all ingredients (ice, too, if you wish) in cocktail mixer and blend well. Serve in highball glass, with ice.

SERVES 1

❧ Mexican Sledgehammer

This is how a boilermaker works, South of the Border.

    1 bottle Mexican beer
    1 ounce tequila

Fill a chilled mug with good Mexican beer. Fill a clean shot glass with tequila. Very carefully lower the full shot glass into the mug. Sip as the two liquors mingle.

SERVES 1

❧ Sangrita

Sangria is a mild fruit punch from Spain, based on red wine. Sangrita, affectionately known as "Devil's Blood," is a brain-stirring drink from Mexico. There are many versions; this echoes the one I sampled long ago on the shores of Lake Chapala. Recalling the orange and red streaks in my glass, I would say it is important not to stir the drink after all the ingredients have been added.

Some aficionados claim the tequila must be sipped first and the remaining ingredients used as a chaser. Not in my book.

    1 teaspoon Worcestershire sauce
    ½ teaspoon salt
    ½ teaspoon finely minced onion
    juice of 1 small lime
    heavy dash grenadine syrup
    4 ounces tequila
    1 cup fresh orange juice
    ½ teaspoon Tabasco or Mexican red-hot sauce

In a highball glass with ice cubes mix all ingredients except the orange juice and Tabasco or other sauce. Stir well. Add the orange juice and stir again. Trickle in the Tabasco or hot sauce and stir very gently so red streaks of "devil's blood" thread through the drink. Sip carefully.

SERVES 1

ꝏ Mexican Chocolate

When Columbus landed in the New World, he discovered Indians who were smoking tobacco and enjoying a thick powerful beverage. The beverage was chocolate, which has since become a world favorite. Aztec chocolate was a strong, sugarless drink, pepped up with chili. It was quaffed by Aztec mailmen before they took off on long-distance runs to deliver messages.

We can enjoy this modern thick and pungent brew without an Olympian sprint. Mexican chocolate makes a great accompaniment to croissants and a light omelet on a frosty Sunday morning. Never resort to baking chocolate if you can obtain a genuine Mexican chocolate bar.

2 ounces baking chocolate or Mexican chocolate
4 cups milk
1 cup sugar
1 teaspoon powdered cinnamon
¼ teaspoon salt
2 eggs
½ teaspoon vanilla

Bring water to a light boil in the lower half of a double boiler. Grate the chocolate into the top half of the double boiler. In a separate pan, heat milk almost to a boil. When chocolate is melted, gradually stir in the hot milk, then the sugar, cinnamon, and salt. Let this cook over the hot water for 20 minutes. Meanwhile, beat the eggs until they are pale and golden, at least 3 minutes. Add a bit of the hot chocolate mixture to the eggs, and stir. Return the eggs to the chocolate mixture, add the vanilla, and beat until frothy. Serve smoking hot.

MAKES 6 CUPS

Mail-Order Sources for Foreign Foods

The stores listed below accept mail orders. It is wise to inquire first if there is a minimum charge. Most of the ingredients mentioned in this book are easily obtainable in any large city; try locally first.

CARIBBEAN, SOUTH AMERICAN, AND MEXICAN

District of Columbia
Pena's Spanish Store
1636 17th Street, N.W.
Washington 20009

Illinois
La Preferida, Inc.
177–181 West South Water
Market
Chicago 60608

Louisiana
Central Grocery Company
923 Decatur Street
New Orleans 70116

Massachusetts
Cardullo's Gourmet Shop
6 Brattle Street
Cambridge 02138

New York
Casa Moneo Spanish Imports
210 West 14th Street
New York 10011

Quebec
Librería Española
3779 St. Dominique Street
Montreal

CHINESE

California
Wing Chong Lung Co.
922 South San Pedro Street
Los Angeles 90015

District of Columbia
Tuck Cheong Company
617 H Street, N.W.
Washington 20001

Wang's
800 Seventh Street, N.W.
Washington 20001

Illinois
Star Market
3349 North Clark Street
Chicago 60657

Massachusetts
  Wing Wing Imported Groceries
  79 Harrison Avenue
  Boston 02111

New York
  Kam Kuo Food Corp.
  7–9 Mott Street
  New York 10013

  Kam Man
  200 Canal Street
  New York 10013

Quebec
  Leong Jung Co., Ltd.
  99 Clark Street
  Montreal

Texas
  Oriental Import-Export
    Company
  2009 Polk Street
  Houston 77003

INDIAN

California
  Haig's Delicacies
  642 Clement Street
  San Francisco 94118

Michigan
  Delmar and Company
  501 Monroe Avenue
  Detroit 48226

New York
  Kalustyan Orient Expert
    Trading Corporation
  123 Lexington Avenue
  New York 10016

Texas
  Antone's
  Box 3352
  Houston 77001

Washington
  House of Rice
  4112 University Way Northeast
  Seattle 98105

INDONESIAN

California
  Holland American Importing Co.
  10343 East Artesia Boulevard
  Bellflower 90706

District of Columbia
  Tuck Cheong Company
  617 H Street, N.W.
  Washington 20001

Illinois
  Mee Jun Emporium
  2223 Wentworth Avenue
  Chicago 60616

New Jersey
  H. Hamstra & Co.
  27 Fairfield Place
  West Caldwell 07006

New York
  Bloomingdale's Delicacies Shop
  Lexington at Fifty-ninth Street
  New York 10028

  Zabar's Gourmet Foods
  2245 Broadway
  New York 10024

Pennsylvania
  Yick Fung Imports
  210 North Ninth Street
  Philadelphia 19107

ITALIAN

Florida
  Joseph Assi's Imported Foods
  3316 Beach Boulevard
  Jacksonville 32207

New York
  Manganaro Brothers
  488 Ninth Avenue
  New York 10018

Tennessee
  Barzizza Bros. Inc.
  4780 Summer Avenue
  P.O. Box 22641
  Memphis 38122

Texas
  Cappello's
  5328 Lemmon Avenue
  Dallas 75209

JAPANESE

California
  Enbun Company
  248 East First Street
  Los Angeles 90012

Colorado
  Pacific Mercantile Company
  1946 Larimer Street
  Denver 80202

Louisiana
  Oriental Merchandise Company
  2636 Edenborn Avenue
  Metairie 70002

Massachusetts
  Yoshinoya
  36 Prospect Street
  Cambridge 02139

New York
  Katagiri Company
  224 East 59th Street
  New York 10022

Ohio
  Soya Food Products
  2356 Wyoming Avenue
  Cincinnati 45214

Quebec
  Miyamoto Provisions
  5997 St. Hubert Street
  Montreal

MIDDLE EASTERN

California
  Mediterranean and Middle East
    Import Company
  233 Valencia Street
  San Francisco 94103

Louisiana
  Progress Grocery Company
  915 Decatur Street
  New Orleans 70116

Massachusetts
  Cardullo's Gourmet Shop
  6 Brattle Street
  Cambridge 02138

Michigan
  American Oriental Grocery
  20736 Lahser Road
  Southfield 48034

Missouri
  Demmas Shish-Ke-Bab
  5806 Hampton Avenue
  St. Louis 63109

New York
  Kalustyan Orient Expert
    Trading Corporation
  123 Lexington Avenue
  New York 10016

  Malko Brothers
  197 Atlantic Avenue
  Brooklyn 11209

SPECIALTY AND SPICE SHOPS

New York
  Bloomingdale's Delicacies Shop
  Lexington Avenue at 59th Street
  New York 10021

  Lekvar by the Barrel
  H. Roth and Son
  1577 First Avenue
  New York 10028

  Maison Glass
  52 East 58th Street
  New York 10022

  Paprikas Weiss
  1546 Second Avenue
  New York 10028

Index

Sauce(s) (*cont'd*)
  Coconut Lemon, Roasted or Barbecued Fish with, 71
  Cumberland, Cocktail Wieners with, 25
  Devil Paste, 240
  Dip
    Spicy, for Fish or Meat, 236
    West Indies, 236
  Dipping, Vietnamese, 234
  Drunk, 225
  fish, notes on, 8
  Greek, A, 232
  Hard, 267
  Harissa, 244
  Horseradish, for Roast Beef, 238
  hot
    Catalonian, 231
    Chinese varieties, 7–8
    general notes on, 8
    North African, 244
    -and-Sweet, 238
  Jalapeño, for Tacos and Enchiladas, 228
  Mohlo de Churrasco, 224
  Mustard, Hungarian, 239
  Nuoc Mam, 234
    notes on, 8
  Oyster, Noodles in, Peking Style, 177
  for pasta. *See* Pasta
  Peanut Butter, Hot, 241
  Pesto alla Genovese, 182
  Piquant, from Mexico, 228
  Piri-Piri 1 and 2, 242
  Skordalia, 232
  Sorrel, 232
  Sour-Cream Horseradish, 237
  Spanish, Basis for, 223
  steak, general notes on, 8
  tomato. *See* Tomatoes
  Tabasco, general notes on, 7
  Vinaigrette, 245
  Walnut, Russian Chicken with, 80
  Wine, for Cooking Fish, 65
  Worcestershire, notes on, 8
  See also Marinades; Salsas
Sauerbraten, 95
Sausage
  Biscuits, 23
  Cheese, Spicy Sicilian, 150
  in Creole Jambalaya, 155

  Hidden, 150
  Homemade, Indian-Style, 148
  Sage, Home-Style, 148
  smoked, in Creole Seafood Gumbo, 66
  in Versteckte Wurst, 151
  See also Chorizo
Seafood
  Gumbo, Creole, 66
  See also Names of fish and shellfish
Seasoning
  Calexico, for Poultry and Meats, 11
  See also Spices
Senegalese Soup, 52
Shellfish. *See* Names of shellfish
Sherry, Pepper, 244
Shigi Yaki, 202
Shortcut Mince Pie, 270
Shrimp
  in Arroz con Pollo, Surinam-Style, 77
  in Creole Seafood Gumbo, 66
  Curry, Trinidad, 68
  in Kan-Shoa Hing-Hsia, 67
  with Mustard Fruits, Four Seasons, 64
  and Tomato, Bahia-Style, 63
  in Vindaloo Curry, 160
  See also Prawns
Sicilian Pepper Cheese Bread, 259
Sicilian Peppers, Potatoes, and Eggs, 188
Skordalia, 232
Sofrito, 223
  notes on, 78
Sole, in Trinidad Steamed Fish, 70
Sopa(s)
  de Ajo, 54
  de Albondigas, 57
Sorrel
  general notes on, 232
  Sauce, 232
Soup(s)
  Bean
    Bayou, 39
    Black, Supreme, 41
    Pinto, 42
  Borani, 56
  Cabbage, Spanish, 59
  Callalou, 43